C000220177

THE INNER CIRCLE

BIRMINGHAM'S NO. 8 BUS ROUTE

IMAGES
of England

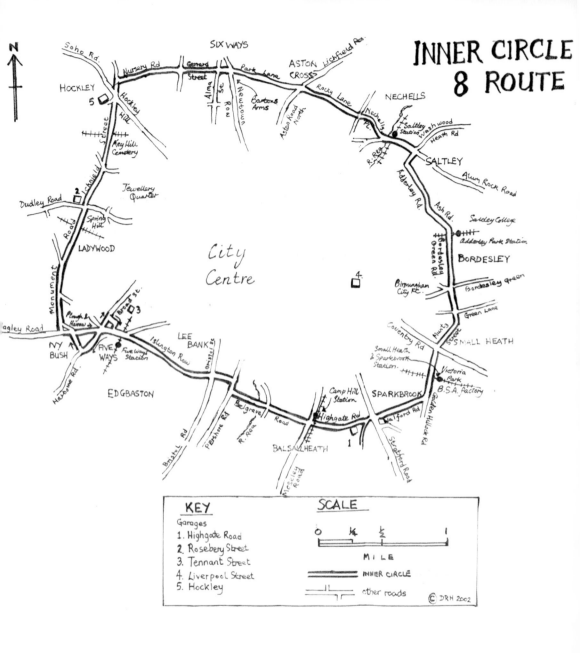

INNER CIRCLE
8 ROUTE

N

Soho Rd.

Nursery Rd.

SIX WAYS

ASTON CROSS

Lichfield Rd.

HOCKLEY

5

General Street

Alma St.

Park Lane

Newtown

Barton's Arms

Rocky Lane

Nechells

NECHELLS

Hockley Hill

K. Newtown

Aston Road North

Nechells Pk.

Saltley Statn

Washwood Heath Rd.

R. Rea

Key Hill Cemetery

Jewellery Quarter

SALTLEY

Alum Rock Road

Dudley Road

2

Icknield Street

Spring Hill

Adderley Rd.

Ash Rd.

Saltley College

Roseberg Road

LADYWOOD

Bordesley Green Rd.

Adderley Park Station

BORDESLEY

City Centre

4

Birmingham City FC.

Bordesley Green

Monument

Broad St.

3

Green Lane

Plough & Harrow

Coventry Rd.

Hurst St.

SMALL HEATH

Bagley Road

FIVE WAYS

Islington Row

LEE BANK

Small Heath & Sparkbrook Station

Victoria Park

IVY BUSH

Five Ways Station

Bristol Rd.

Small Heath

B.S.A. Factory

Harborne Rd.

EDGBASTON

Belgrave Road

Camp Hill Station

SPARKBROOK

Golden Hillock Rd.

Pershore Rd.

R. Rea

Highgate Rd.

Walford Rd.

Strafford Road

BALSALL HEATH

Moseley Road

1

KEY

Garages
1. Highgate Road
2. Rosebery Street
3. Tennant Street
4. Liverpool Street
5. Hockley

SCALE

0   ¼   ½   1

MILE

INNER CIRCLE

other roads

© DRH 2002

IMAGES
of England

THE INNER CIRCLE
BIRMINGHAM'S NO. 8 BUS ROUTE

Margaret Hanson, David Harvey and Peter Drake

TEMPUS

A cartoon reproduced from the *Birmingham Tramways Gazette,* the official magazine of the Birmingham Corporation Tramway and Omnibus Department, Social Athletics and Thrift Society.

First published 2002, reprinted 2003

Tempus Publishing Limited
The Mill, Brimscombe Port,
Stroud, Gloucestershire, GL5 2QG

© Margaret Hanson, David Harvey and Peter Drake, 2002

The right of Margaret Hanson, David Harvey and Peter Drake to be identified as the authors
of this work has been asserted by them in accordance with the
Copyrights, Designs and Patents Act 1988.

All rights reserved. No part of this book may be reprinted
or reproduced or utilised in any form or by any electronic,
mechanical or other means, now known or hereafter invented,
including photocopying and recording, or in any information
storage or retrieval system, without the permission in writing
from the Publishers.

British Library Cataloguing in Publication Data.
A catalogue record for this book is available from the British Library.

ISBN 0 7524 2636 2

Typesetting and origination by Tempus Publishing Limited
Printed in Great Britain by Midway Colour Print, Wiltshire

Contents

Preface

The photographs in this book have come from two main sources. Nearly every photograph featuring a No. 8 bus has come from the private collection of David Harvey, and most of these are being reproduced for the first time. The photographs of buildings and street scenes have come from the collections of the Local Studies section of the Birmingham Central Reference Library, where they can be easily accessed. In turn, the library's collections have been built up from a variety of donations from individuals, from the City Council's own planning and engineers department and from special commissions. The up-to-date views were taken by a local photographer, Barbara Palmer, and these images have been added to the Central Library's collections.

Acknowledgements

The compilers are grateful to the many photographers who have contributed to this volume. In particular they would like to thank Roger Carpenter, Barry Ware and Linda Chew from the Birmingham Co-op History Group. Unless otherwise stated all the photographs are from the collections in Birmingham Central Library.

From the Central Library we would like to thank Chris Ash, Joe McKenna and Steve Haste for their companionship on trips round the route. Thanks as well to Martin Flynn for commissioning the book. From West Midlands Travel Richard Kirk and Margaret Winthrop have been helpful. The hosts and customers of The Queens Arms and The Gunmakers, including the wonderful Sonny, should be thanked both for their hospitality and their local knowledge, as well as Tina and Paul Archer of the Model Inn, Oldbury, for their tolerance and excellent real ale. Thanks also to Pat Johnson and Bernard Jackson. Finally, thanks are also due to Diane Harvey for proof-reading the initial draft.

Introduction

The complete Inner Circle bus route was first operated on 8 February 1928 and has operated continuously ever since. The Inner Circle, No. 8 route, has carried on operating despite the Second World War, numerous road changes and over seventy years of social change in the city and continues to provide a transport service linking Birmingham's inner suburbs. When the service was started it was an immediate success and reached the height of its popularity in the 1950s. It was always one of Birmingham City Transport's most profitable and frequent bus services. The Inner Circle was always known as the 'Workmen's Special' because of the number of factories along or very close to the route. People would jump on the No. 8 to go to the nearest shops, to go to the local cinema or even the next pub down the road. It was the bus service for the real 'Brummie', who didn't have to go 'into town' to find food, entertainment or work. Thus it became one of the busiest routes in the city, characterized by large numbers of short distance passengers. Many of the city's best-known businesses such as Lucas, Ansells Brewery, HP Sauce, B.S.A. and Bulpitts were on the route and rush hours saw the No. 8 ferrying what seemed like most of the city's workforce to and from the factory gates. Several of the areas through which the buses travelled had smaller factories and workshops, almost jostling side by side with the very houses lived in by the factory workers.

Most of the factories which lined the route were subsequently demolished, but it had been their workers who for years had provided the service with its peak hour 'bread and butter' revenue. The majority of the 'all-day' passengers who used the Inner Circle bus route were those who lived on or near the route itself, living in the swathes of Victorian back-to-back houses, courtyards, terraces and even the one-time high quality villas which stood within a short walk of this important inter-suburban bus service. The removal of these old houses took their former inhabitants away to new estates such as Bromford Bridge, Hawkesley, Frankley and Chelmsley Wood and with them went many of the passengers who used the Inner Circle. This depopulation was further exacerbated by the construction of sections of the Middleway which cut further holes in the bus route's Victorian catchment areas.

Today, it is less used as shown by fewer buses on the route and by the gradual replacement of double-deckers by single-deckers. The route has had a fascinating history, much of which is still visible from the windows of the No. 8. The Inner Circle has never had its devotees in the way that the No. 11, the famous Outer Circle, has had, always appearing to be the poor cousin. The No. 11 has been promoted for its tourist potential, but no one has thought along the same lines with the poor old Inner Circle. Hopefully, the publication of this book may start off a revival of interest in Birmingham's surviving legacy along this most interesting of routes.

It is fascinating to travel back three-quarters of a century to the start of the service in order to recreate such a different city and such a different bus service. It was not merely the buses themselves which belong to this vanished era. The operation of the vehicles was very different from today. There were the drivers who were still wearing knee-length leather boots; there were also conductors of course, one-person-operated buses only starting on the route in June 1971. Instead of radios and

CCTV, the equipment the crews carried was of a slightly less sophisticated nature. It consisted of a rope, a spark plug, matches and a candle. The spark plug could be warmed by the candle, which in turn was lit by the matches, while the rope was needed to start the engine. In these early days the buses were feeling their way against trams, which in Birmingham, at least, held the upper hand until, strangely, about the same date as the Inner Circle bus service began. It was a different age in which conductors would actually escort children off their bus and up to the front doors of their homes. Traffic was obviously very much lighter in the pre-war period; it was not until the 1950s that the numbers of motorcars began to increase dramatically, which gradually reduced the numbers of bus passengers. Some of the earliest complaints about the operation of the service which reached the letters pages of The Birmingham Mail were commenting on the excessive speed reached by some No. 8 bus drivers.

The Changes in the Modern Inner Circle Route Today

The redevelopment of the inner city suburbs in the 1960s has dramatically changed the character, operational requirements and even the line of the route. Birmingham has a reputation for never letting its road system stay the same for too long and this is reflected along the Inner Circle route. The Middle Ring Road was begun in the early 1960s, though it took until 1998 to complete. The road changed most of the western side of the Inner Circle route through Ladywood and Balsall Heath. The creation of the Middle Ring Road was essentially part of the city's response to the expansion in car ownership which was effectively snarling up the arterial approaches to and from the city centre. Other route alterations, because of changed passenger needs, have affected the Inner Circle service throughout its ten mile journey. Some recent alterations to the route have taken place, such as the diversion through the Jewellery Quarter and the evening and Sunday re-routing of the service to take in the city's newest entertainment complex at Star City.

The No. 8 route no longer travels along narrow streets with back-to-backs, courtyard and tunnel-back terraces leading off roads such as Muntz Street, Sun Street, Park Lane and Belgrave Road. The traditional corner shops have largely disappeared, while in Icknield Street old public houses such as The Gate, The Mint, The Bulls Head and The Great Western Inn have all been demolished. Even the cinemas directly on the route, such as The Waldorf in Walford Road have gone while occupying the site of the once hugely popular ABC in Bristol Road is a drive-through McDonalds. Another long gone cinema is The Ladywood Picture House, which stood in Ledsam Street, just off Monument Road. This was originally opened in 1910 to provide cheap entertainment in this once bustling residential and shopping area. Not long after the arrival of 'The Talkies' it was modernised and re-opened in 1932 as The New Regent. The last film was shown in 1959 before it was demolished to make way for Ladywood Middleway. In fact, the only cinema on the route today is at the recently constructed Star City leisure complex and that is nearly one mile away from the original line of the old Inner Circle.

Even on those parts of the route which have avoided wholesale change, the 'look' of the Inner Circle's urban landscape has altered dramatically. Perhaps the best example of this changed environment, in microcosm, is to catch the 8C, (the C meaning clockwise around the city, while the 8A was the anticlockwise Inner Circle), from Hockley flyover. As the bus turns away from Hockley, it goes into Hunters Road before turning into Nursery Street and its eastward bound extension of Gerrard Street, which will take the passenger to Wheeler Street at the edge of Lozells. It leaves behind an Indian Community Centre in Hockley, housed in the former Icknield Street School, before passing through a remnant of the original late Victorian terraced houses which at one time covered this area. The replacement 1960s houses already look their age but there are still two thriving and friendly nineteenth-century corner pubs, The Union and The Gunmakers Arms, (unfortunately stripped by thieves during the refurbishment of its magnificent bar). In this short stretch of the route, there are still some factories and small industrial units, while there is also the local Mayfield J & I school, Lozells Methodist church, a housing development built for the local West Indian community, a convent and a Bangladeshi Advice Centre. All this in two-thirds of a mile!

Despite, or perhaps because of, these changes, a tour of the No. 8 route is a fascinating experience for anyone who is interested in the history of the city. Crossing Five Ways and Aston Cross, the bus passes two of the city's most historic spots with a range of old and new buildings. In Newtown, the contrast between the old and new is wonderfully shown by the fortune of two pubs, the magnificently tiled Barton's Arms and the sixties-built Shareholders Arms. At the bottom of Dudley Road stands the wonderfully restored Spring Hill Library, built in 1893, which stands cheek-by-jowl with the recently demolished 1960s-built Brookfield shopping precinct, that represents all that was bad with 1960s town planning and redevelopment. Places of worship reflect the diverse nature of modern Birmingham, with the impressive Central Mosque building in Belgrave Middleway, which was built, somewhat ironically, on the site of Dares Brewery. The Inner Circle route also takes in Gudwaras, Sikh Temples, the Hockley Pentecostal Church, with its boldly advertised messages to believers and the splendid Perpendicular-styled St Saviours Church in Saltley, which dates from 1849. Stop and explore the early nineteenth-century splendour of the Jewellery Quarter and visit the two cemeteries at Key Hill and Warstone Lane where some of the famous and good founding fathers of Birmingham are buried, while as a total contrast, the Inner Circle bus passes across Ladypool Road in Sparkbrook, which is the centre of the famous 'Balti' belt. Birmingham's attempt to host top-class street motor racing, known as the Super Prix, took place over part of the Inner Circle route, though one doubts if a Daimler 'Fleetline' or a Mark II Metrobus had the same top speed as a MacLaren Formula 3000 racing car! A final contrast must be in Nechells where the seventies miner's strike had its most dramatic confrontation leading to the coal miners of the N.U.M. having their greatest moment of brief political glory.

The Buses on the Route

Since 1928, there have been many changes to the service, to the route and to the districts along the route. For most of the Inner Circle's service life, only a few Corporation bus garages regularly worked on the service. Initially, it was Tennant Street garage which operated the open-toppers, but once Barford Street was opened, the majority of the low-height A.D.C. 507s used on the No. 8 route were operated from here. Although Birchfield Road garage briefly did turns on the Inner Circle from 1935 to 1936, the opening of Liverpool Street garage in Deritend in September 1936 began a tradition which continues today, although the garage is now called Birmingham Central. After their respective tram service abandonments, Highgate Road, in 1937, Hockley in 1939 and Rosebery Street, after 1947, all did turns on the Inner Circle. Each garage operated different types of buses which added to the variety on the service and made a ride round seem all the more interesting.

The development of the buses themselves has a fascinating history all of its own. The first section of the route was opened on 17 February 1926 from The Gate at Saltley via Bordesley Green to Stratford Road, while on the following 16 August, the service was extended via Highgate Road, Lee Bank, Five Ways, Icknield Street to Hockley, when the incomplete 'circle' was first given the name 'Inner Circle'. It was at this time that the buses used were open-topped A.E.C.503s with fifty-four seat bodies built by the Brush Company of Loughborough. Operated from Barford Street, as they approached the former Great Western Railway's bridge at Icknield Street, the bus would be draw up to a halt and the conductor would climb the outside staircase and tell all the upper saloon passengers to stay in their seats while the bus passed through the long, dark depths of the bridge.

The first buses bought specifically for the new service were twenty-five A.D.C. 507s with low-height, top-covered, outside staircase bodies built by the aircraft builder, Short Brothers, which entered service in June 1927. With their twenty upper saloon seats, arranged in 'herring-bone' fashion with two side gangways, they were nicknamed 'pick-pocket specials'. They were low-bridge in order to get under the bridges in Icknield Street and at Highgate Road. The full circle was completed on 8 February 1928 from Hockley, via Aston Cross to Saltley and in August 1928, a further ten A.D.C. 507s were purchased, but all were destined to have short lives being replaced by more modern, standardised buses in 1934. After this, the next new type of bus to be used on the service was the Gardner 5LW Diesel-powered, Daimler COG5, with locally built bodies manufactured by Metro-Cammell of Saltley or Birmingham Railway, Carriage and Wagon from Oldbury. The Daimler was to be the standard double-decker in Birmingham's bus fleet from 1934 until 1940, although a few turns on the Inner Circle were undertaken by the unique Leyland 'Titan TD6cs with their torque convertor gearboxes, from Hockley garage.

During the Second World War, both Liverpool Street and Barford Street operated wartime Guy 'Arab' Mk IIs on the service which had a variety of standardised-looking bodies built by a number of different body manufacturers to what has been termed 'Utility' design. Many had wooden-slatted seating, all had a limited number of opening windows and all suffered from premature body defects because of the poor quality wood which was used in their body construction. The last ones lingered on until 1951, while most of the pre-war bus stock had been cleared out some three years later. What replaced this motley crew of elderly buses were the magnificent Daimler CVG6s with Metro-Cammell bodies built between 1947 and 1949, which operated from both Highgate Road, Barford Street and Liverpool Street garages. Registered in the GOE series or with HOV registrations, these buses slogged their way around the Inner Circle for nearly twenty reliable years, leading to the old parody 'HOV bus, will travel' - remember 'Gunsmoke'? From about 1950 onwards Liverpool Street supported the Inner Circle with a variety of exposed radiator and 'New-Look fronted Crossley DD42/7s with Crossley bodies, while throughout the 1950s and 1960s, Hockley garage supplied the route with Leyland-bodied Leyland 'Titan' PD2/1s, while the nearby Rosebery Street used buses with the same body but with non-standard Park Royal bodywork. The advent of the trolleybus and tram replacement buses between 1951 and 1953 saw the last of the Daimler CVD6, with Daimler CD6 engines operating from Liverpool Street, Hockley and Rosebery Street, while the slightly later Crossley-bodied Daimler CVG6s in the JOJ registration series came from Barford Street, Liverpool Street and Highgate Road. Slightly later, identical buses in the MOF registration group were also to be found on the Inner Circle service being operated by Hockley garage.

Occasionally oddments, like three of the unusually-styled Park Royal-bodied A.E.C.'Regent' IIIs, temporarily allocated to Barford Street to test air-brakes on a high intensity route with lots of starting and stopping, appeared on the Inner Circle. From about the time of the closure of Barford Street garage in April 1955, the service settled down for about sixteen years using the same batches of buses. Even the operating garages remained the same for the No. 8 routes. It was only the advent of the Daimler 'Fleetline' in about 1964 which began to alter the vehicles that were regularly seen on the route. The Inner Circle continued to be the preserve of the standard B.C.T. front-engined double-decker until the end of 1968. Towards the end of Corporation operation, various batches of the rear-engined 'Fleetlines' began to appear regularly on the Inner Circle and at the very end of Birmingham's municipal operation a batch of buses were ordered specifically to work on the No. 8. Nicknamed the 'Jumbos', these 33' long Park Royal-bodied 80 seater Daimler 'Fleetlines', with their dual-doors, proved to be too tall to pass safely under the 14' 6' high Icknield Street bridge. Quickly, the previous batch of NOV——G registered 'Fleetlines' were substituted and the too tall SOE —-H registered 'Jumbos' were put to work on the gruelling services along Bristol Road to Rednal and Rubery. Since the demise of Corporation operation, the route has seen a variety of Daimler/Leyland 'Fleetlines' and after 1980, both Mark I and Mark II M.C.W. 'Metrobuse' have seen all day service on the Inner Circle. Even today, when 43-seater Mercedes-Benz 0405Ns work the all-day turns on the Inner Circle, 'Metrobuses' are still operated on the Inner Circle and defying the worries of their upstairs front passengers as the bus ducks beneath the girders of Highgate Road bridge, seemingly just before the top deck seems bound to hit the bridge.

Final Thought

As Hillary Burde, the hero of Iris Murdoch's novel A Word Child puts it , 'I loved the Inner Circle best... sometimes I rode the whole circle'. Enjoy this book and its photographs, but also make the effort to enjoy the journey on the top deck of a No. 8 bus. We hope that this book will inspire you to do that because it will be an hour and twenty minutes well spent.

One
The Buses

Twenty-five of these low-height buses were ordered in 1927 and another ten in 1928. These were A.D.C. 507s with Short L20/26 RO bodies and were required in order to allow buses with top covers beneath the low bridges in Icknield Street, Hockley and Highgate Road, Balsall Heath. They had enclosed cabs and were among the first to have pneumatic tyres. On the upper saloon were bucket seats arranged in herring-bone fashion over the raised central lower saloon ceiling. With only twenty bucket seats and a gangway on either side of the saloon, they became known as 'pickpocket specials'. Access to the upper saloon was by way of an external staircase. These thirty-five buses revolutionized the Inner Circle service, however, all were withdrawn by 1934, by which time the roads had been lowered sufficiently to allow normal buses. (D.R. Harvey Collection)

This is the type of double-decker that was first employed on the newly opened sections of the infant Inner Circle bus route, but isn't actually working on the route. 66 (OK 8008), is in Harborne, near the Duke of York public house, during the 1926 General Strike. There are a number of policemen in evidence who are there to protect the volunteer bus crews, many of whom were students from the nearby University of Birmingham. The drivers are receiving instruction on how to drive these A.E.C. 503. 66 had an open-top fifty-four seater body which was built by Brush Engineering of Loughborough, entering service on 8 May 1923. 66 survived until September 1930 when it was converted to a mobile welding van. (D.R. Harvey Collection)

Opposite: A short-lived demonstrator which was tried out on the Inner Circle bus route was the fourth Dennis 'Lance' to be built. Numbered 93, PL 3078 was on extended loan from 7 March to 15 May 1931 and is pictured in Barford Street near to the garage in its nearly all-over dark blue livery. The manufacturer of the body on the bus has always been attributed to a bodybuilder called 'Westgate', but as the bus was sold to the Earlswood Bus Company of Westgate-on-Sea, the origin of the H27/24R body is still something of a mystery. It does look as though it might have been built by Brush. (D.R. Harvey Collection)

Parked outside the offices in Highgate Road garage in 1959 are two similar buses, which are fulfilling two very different purposes. On the left, with the destination blinds, is a well-varnished Daimler COG5, 1096 (CVP 196), of 1937 vintage, which was given a repaint in 1958; this was when the Corporation were short of buses after taking over services from Midland Red in the north side of the city. 893 (BOP 893), another Metro-Cammell bodied COG5, but this time dating from 1936, was withdrawn in 1954 and although outlasting 1096 by three years, was converted to a snowplough in November 1954 and by this time, the bus was allocated to Highgate Road garage. Careful examination shows the bus is fitted with chains on the rear tyres and under the bus is a snowplough, just visible where the lifeguard should be. (A.B. Cross)

With the snow reflected off the highly varnished dark blue paintwork, 1019 (CVP 119), manoeuvres in Queen Street in the winter of 1958. This Metro-Cammell bodied Daimler COG5, fitted with the usual Gardner 5LW 7.0 litre diesel engine, entered service on 1 July 1937. 1019 would only work out of Highgate Road garage for twenty-one months, usually on shortworkings, before it was delicensed. (L.Mason)

This bus is a 'Gearless' Leyland! When it became obvious that the pre-war tram abandonment would outstrip the ability for Daimlers to produce sufficient buses for B.C.T., Birmingham bought five A.E.C.s and five Leylands in 1937 to compare. The winner was Leyland Motors, which was to be a 'Titan' model but which was fitted with a torque converter gearbox. Before the vehicles were ordered, the corporation engineers required a chassis which had their modifications. The result was the 'Titan' TD6c, of which 135 were built in 1938 and 1939, uniquely all for Birmingham. The first 85 had M.C.C.W. bodies which seated only fifty-two, as the weight of the torque converter made the bus overweight with a full load of passengers. 242 (EOG 242), with an M.C.C.W. body, passes along Whitmore Street, running empty back to Hockley garage in about 1953. (R. Marshall)

The bombing of Hockley garage destroyed the bodies of eighteen buses, of these twelve had their chassis salvaged and were eventually rebodied, with English Electric H28/26R 'streamlined' bodies which were intended for Manchester corporation. One of these was 217 (EOG 217), which was a Leyland 'Titan' TD6c, which originally looked like 242. In September 1949, 217 is standing on the forecourt of Hockley garage, which still has its cobbles and the remnants of the tram tracks last used in May 1939. Behind the bus is the nineteenth-century factory of John Rabone & Sons who made rulers and spirit levels. The road behind the bus, containing three-storey courtyard Victorian back-to-backs is Ford Street which had on its corner for many years the coffee rooms of Mrs Browning, used extensively by the mechanics and platform staff of Hockley garage. (R. Knibbs/D.R. Harvey collection)

The last fifty Leyland 'Titan' TD6Cs had Leyland's own bodywork, which coupled to the requirements of straight staircase, standard Birmingham interior fixtures and fittings and the external mouldings and beading, produced possibly the best looking of all Birmingham's pre-war double-deckers. The 1270-1319 class were purchased to replace the Dudley Road tramcars and as a result, they were allocated to Hockley garage where they augmented the earlier EOG-registered batch. In later years, most of these buses were transferred to Rosebery Street garage, though 1316 (FOF 316), which had entered service on 1 November 1939, waits opposite Hockley garage about eighteen months before its withdrawal which occurred until 31 October 1953. (R. Marshall)

The back streets of Balsall Heath was the location of Barford Street garage. In 1946, the garage received a handful of wartime Guy 'Arab' IIs from Liverpool Street to help out on their two operated services, the City Circle, 19, and the Inner Circle, 8. 1407 (FOP 407), a Park Royal-bodied bus, which was originally fitted with wooden slatted seats, is parked just short of the entrance to the garage with, just inside the door, an unidentified pre-war Daimler COG5 and a post-war Daimler CVG6. The combination of these three buses being seen at Barford Street would suggest that this is 1949 or early 1950, as 1407 would be taken out of service in June 1950. (D.R. Harvey collection)

Opposite: Standing at the Bundy Clock in Adderley Road in the autumn of 1953 is an exposed radiator Crossley DD42/7 with a fifty-four seat Crossley body. The bus is 2415 (JOJ 415), which was new on 1 June 1950 and would last in service for fifteen years. The Crossley-engined buses were among the heaviest to enter service with B.C.T., weighing in at 8 tons 7 cwt 1 qrt. On the wall of the mean Victorian shops is an advertisement for the nearby Rock cinema which is showing the 1952 film *My Cousin Rachel*, which was based on the Daphne du Maurier novel and starred Olivier de Havilland and Richard Burton. Suburban cinemas would receive the 'big' films many months after their release. (K. Lane)

Right: The post-war shortage of buses meant that Birmingham bought fifty 'off-the-peg' Leyland-bodied Leyland 'Titan' PD2/1s. These powerful 9.8 litre engined buses were all allocated to Hockley garage and were used quite regularly on the Inner Circle. They were only about 14' high and as a result cleared the Icknield Street and Highgate Road railway bridges more easily than any other class of Birmingham's buses. With a very low weight of 7 tons 10cwt 3qts, these buses were among the fastest in the B.C.T. fleet, but were not popular away from their more normal haunts along Soho Road, because they did not have straight staircases, unlike the equivalent pre-war FOF-registered TD6cs. 2152 (JOJ 152) is parked on the forecourt of Hockley garage when still fairly new as it still has the original thin central blue band with which it was delivered. (D.R. Harvey)

One class of buses which were undoubtedly the stalwarts of the Inner Circle route were the HOV-registered Daimler CVG6s, numbered 1844-1930. These Metro-Cammell-bodied buses were built between 1948 and 1949 and lasted in service for nineteen or twenty years. 1861 (HOV 861), speeds past the early 1950s flats of the Lee Bank Comprehensive Development Area at the bottom of Sun Street West. The bus is approaching the Bristol Street crossing in about 1964. These buses, with their pre-selector, fluid flywheel gearboxes and Gardner 8.4 litre engines were admirably suited to day-after-day slogging around the 8 route, being operated by Barford Street, Highgate Road and Liverpool Street garages, with 1861 spending all its long life at the latter two garages. There were 87 in this batch and by Birmingham standards, they achieved very high mileages, with most of those which remained in service until 1968, topping well over 600,000 miles. These buses tended to run rather hot and as such were nicknamed 'pot-boilers'. (A.D. Broughall)

The first class of buses delivered with the Birmingham developed 'New Look' front, which hid the radiator behind a bulbous bonnet, were the last batch of 100 Crossley DD42/7s to be delivered to the corporation. 2438 (JOJ 438), is crossing Stratford Road in Sparkbrook from Walford Road on a short working of the Inner Circle which would turn back at Sherlock Street. These buses with their synchromesh gearboxes were harder work for the drivers who were more used to vehicles with pre-selector gearboxes. This bus, with its heavyweight Crossley body, was one of the earlier withdrawals, being taken out of service in October 1968, but most lasted into the first three months of the following year, including the preserved example, 2489, (JOJ 489) owned by one of the authors. (D.R. Harvey Collection)

Above: Some of the most attractive looking post-war buses which were bought by the corporation were fifty buses that were, unusually, not built to B.C.T.'s specifications. Although the Park Royal bodied Leyland 'Titan' PD2/1s were garaged at both Hockley and Rosebery Street for about eighteen years, they were infrequent performers on the Inner Circle route as their unusual staircase layout was unfamiliar for most of the potential passengers. On 20 September 1961, in Islington Row, 2228 (JOJ 228), was working on the 8 route, travelling towards Five Ways. (J. Carroll)

One of the extremely quiet, but oil-burning Daimler-engined Daimler CVD6s waits outside the Brewer's Arms in Highgate Road while its crew wait to 'peg the clock' during 1953. The bus, 2713 (JOJ 713), has retained all its decorative wheel discs and has gained the clip immediately below the front destination box which was used in June 1953 for fitting two celebratory Coronation flags. These Metro-Cammell bodied buses were the first to have one-piece bodies, rather than a separate upper and lower decks, were one foot longer than any of the previous buses and also had deeper saloon windows. (S.N.J. White)

Left: Towards the middle of 1968, with large numbers of new rear-engined Daimler 'Fleetline' entering service, there was a series of vehicle transfers which put some of the heavyweight, short length Guy 'Arab' III Specials onto the Inner Circle route for the first time. 2569 (JOJ 569), was one of the 100 M.C.C.W. bodied 'Arabs' and was first licensed on 1 December 1950, remaining in service until early 1972, by which time it was owned by West Midlands P.T.E. Here, 2569 is crossing Bristol Street from Belgrave Road on its way towards Five Ways in 1969, with the newly completed Matthew Boulton College standing like a chessboard on the right above the Austin LD van. (R.F. Mack)

Travelling along Islington Row in about 1958, having just passed Tennant Street with the Shell and BP petrol station on the corner, is 2783 (JOJ 783). It is 'surrounded' by German built cars, which at the time was quite unusual. In front of it is a Volkswagen Beetle, and it is being followed by what appears to be an Opel. This was one of the first of a batch of 125 Daimler CVG6s with Crossley H30/25R bodies, built to the new 27' 6" length which entered service in July 1952. Initially this bus was used on the Bristol Road routes to replace the tramcar service to Rednal and Rubery. Although slightly lighter than the contemporary Metro-Cammell bodied Guy 'Arab' IVs, nearly all of these vehicles would survive into P.T.E. ownership, with 2783 lasting until January 1975. (R.H.G. Simpson)

This Crossley-bodied Daimler CVG6 had a strange after-life as it was sold to two Frenchmen in December 1973 and was driven to its final resting place as a roadside snackbar on Route Nationale 44, two kilometres south-east of Laon on the road to Rheims. But that was four years in the future – in 1969, 3164 (MOF 164), a bus which had entered service on 1 March 1954 as one of the second batch of 125 Crossley-bodied CVG6s, turns out of High Street, Saltley, in front of The Gate public house as it turns into Adderley Road, prior to clocking in at the Bundy clock. (A. Yates)

When, in 1963, B.C.T. purchased their first large batch of rear-engined double-deckers, they chose the Coventry-manufactured Daimler 'Fleetline' CRG6LX model. The body building order for the first 100 was split between Washwood Heath-produced Metro-Cammell and London-based Park Royal. Both produced a somewhat uninspired flat-fronted body design which carried seventy-two passengers. 3346 (346 GON), by now in P.T.E. ownership, is displaying that most typical of Birmingham destinations, SERVICE EXTRA as it travels along the wasteland that was Muntz Street not long after the rows of Victorian terraced houses had been demolished. (Travel Lens)

Muntz Street, Small Heath, as it used to be. Muntz Street was named after George Frederick Muntz who was the Liberal MP for Birmingham from 1840 until his death in 1857 and who had perfected the process of perforating postage stamps. The Muntz family were of Polish origin and made their fortune from the manufacture of metal bolts and nails. 3694 (KOX 694), a Daimler 'Fleetline' with a Metro-Cammell body of a later design and an attractively designed 'V' shaped front windscreen, is travelling towards Coventry Road on the 8 route in May 1970, though apparently still in full corporation livery. (F.W. York)

The last buses introduced onto the Inner Circle bus route in corporation days were forty-eight dual-doored Daimler 'Fleetline' CRG6LXs with Park Royal bodywork. 3819 (NOV 819G) waits in Highgate Road in 1969, opposite the Brewer's Arms and between the Queen's Arms on the corner of Queen Street, which the bus is facing towards and, on the corner of Stoney Lane, the Lion and Lamb public house. These buses were the first to be built specifically for one-man operation. They had separate entrance and exit doors and centre staircases which was supposed to increase loading and unloading speeds. As the centre door could only be operated when the bus was out of gear, these buses constantly lost time because these advances made them much slower. These two-door buses were not suitable for the extremely busy Inner Circle. (L. Mason)

The last buses bought for the Inner Circle were 100 thirty-three foot long Daimler 'Fleetline' CRG6LX s with Park Royal H47/33D bodies. These, as far as the 8 bus route is concerned, were the great 'might have beens'. Unfortunately the 'Jumbos', as they were nicknamed, were slightly taller than the standard 14' 4½" and on a trial run it was considered that they were too close to the underside of Icknield Street bridge. As a result the majority of the class were allocated to Selly Oak garage to work the services along Bristol Road. On 16 September 1969, two weeks before the P.T.E. took over Birmingham's municipal bus fleet, 3882 (SOE 882H), one of only two to receive full B.C.T. livery and crests, turns into Yardley Wood garage at the end of a driver familiarization journey. (L. Mason)

Two

The Circle Starts:
Five Ways to Bristol Road

Under the benign presence of Joseph Sturge, two ladies, one carrying a well-wrapped infant, stride out from the corner of Ladywood Road as they begin to cross Five Ways. Joseph Sturge was the archetypal Victorian philanthropist with his 'practical benevolence towards men in general'. Even in about 1924, the traffic around Five Ways had its own 'gyratory' system. The tram tracks in the foreground takes the 33 tram to Ladywood from Islington Row on the left, while on the far side of the statue are both tracks for the 34 route along Hagley Road. The bus standing in Calthorpe Road is a Daimler Y-type of 1916 vintage, which had been rebodied in 1922 by Christopher Dodson. Buses of this type might have briefly worked on the new and as yet incomplete Inner Circle route. (Birmingham Central Reference Library)

Pulling away from the impressive bus stops in Harborne Road is one of the work horses of the Inner Circle route. 1894 (HOV 894), an exposed radiatored Daimler CVG6 with a Metro-Cammell fifty-four seat body, is working away from Five Ways on its way towards the Ivy Bush on 11 February 1968. This nineteen-year-old bus had only just over six weeks in service left before it was withdrawn. Towering over the redevelopment work which was being undertaken at this time in the Five Ways area is the multi-storied Auchinleck House, designed by J. Seymour Harris Partnership, which was begun in 1964 and named after the Second World War General Sir Claude Auchinleck. (B.W. Ware)

In the 1950s, the Five Ways junction was a far different place to the huge traffic island and underpass of today, still having the old boundary stone between Birmingham and Edgbaston. Speeding from Five Ways into Harborne Road, with Newbury's carpet cleaning shop on the far side of Hagley Road is 2713 (JOJ 713). This Daimler CVD6 had a fifty-four seater Metro-Cammell body and entered service on 1 September 1951. In this 1957 view, the bus has lost its decorative wheel discs, but retains its semaphore trafficators, while Five Ways remains unaltered, though the demolition ball and chain was only five years away. (W.J. Haynes)

Joseph Sturge, the Victorian philanthropist whose statue stands proudly at the Five Ways. A Birmingham corn merchant and Quaker he is best remembered for his campaigns against slavery. His portrait also adorns the Round Room in the Birmingham Museum and Art Gallery. As a Quaker, Sturge disapproved of music, condemning it as 'unfavourable to the health of the soul', so it is rather ironic that his statue now faces the musical hub of Birmingham, Broad Street, with its numerous clubs.

Sturge's memorial in front of the Marriott Hotel. The only example of public art on the inner circle route and Birmingham's only monument to cultural diversity – one of the figures shows Charity holding a black child, a reference to Sturge's anti-slavery work. The memorial, by the London sculptor, John Thomas, was unveiled on 4 June 1862, three years after Sturge's death, in front of 12,000 spectators.

Above: B.C.T. was one of the earliest municipalities to specify an 'easy change' gearbox and therefore became very interested in Leyland Motors' 'gearless transmission', which used Lysholm-Smith patents. Eventually, the corporation purchased five Leyland 'Titan' TD4cs which had Leyland's own Colin Bailey-designed metal-framed bodies. Bailey had been 'head-hunted' from Metro-Cammell in Saltley to design a second metal-framed double-decker, as the previous one, introduced in September 1933, had been a disaster. The first of the Bailey-designed Leyland bodies was built in March 1936 and 964 (COX 964), Birmingham's first example, was delivered on 1 May 1937. Here it is turning out of Islington Row in May 1938, with the Five Ways clock showing five to three. To the right is the white Portland stone faced Lloyd Bank building in Calthorpe Road, which was opened in 1909 to the design of P.B. Chatwin and still survives today. (D.R. Harvey Collection)

Immediately before the Second World War, the land between George Street and Frederick Street was cleared for the proposed new BBC studios, to replace those in Broad Street. Although the land was cleared, the scheme was postponed because of the war, with the BBC moving to Pebble Mill in the mid-1960s. In 1957 construction work began on the Islington Row site with a development called Five Ways House, which was designed by the Ministry of Works architects to a somewhat repetitive design. It was originally occupied by the Municipal Estates Department and later by offices of the civil service. Parked on the cleared land is an Austin 10/4 whose bonnet is covered by a rug, while coming out of Tennant Street is another Austin Seven Ruby, which is followed by a Rover 12 or 14 of about 1937 and a large Wolseley saloon. The Anchor Inn, with its decorative bar windows, stood on the opposite corner of Islington Row and Tennant Street. This thriving Victorian-built pub was demolished in 1965 to make way for the unloved Five Ways shopping centre. Tennant Street had been the first site of the corporation's bus fleet, having taken over the garage premises from Midland Red. (Birmingham Central Reference Library)

Opposite: The Inner Circle bus turns out of Islington Row and into Calthorpe Road, *c.* 1961. The whole of the Five Ways junction was still controlled by traffic lights. The clock tower opposite the National Provincial Bank has been moved, while in the 1890s buildings behind the bus, are Susan Hancock's fruit and vegetable shop and, with its canvas blinds pulled down, Whittaker's furniture store. The castellated Art Nouveaux buildings in Islington Row, on the extreme right, were all replaced by the Auchinleck Square development of 1964. The junction at Five Ways was perhaps the most prestigious on the Inner Circle bus route, having the then more commercial and administrative Broad Street meeting the carefully regulated Calthorpe Estate at the old boundary with Edgbaston. The bus is a 1949 Daimler CVG6 1885 (HOV 885), which would be converted into a snowplough in November 1963, surviving until the summer of 1971 having hardly turned a wheel for nearly eight years. (A.D. Broughall)

29

Although Islington Row still looked like a building site, it was September 1970 and the reconstruction of the Five Ways area and Islington Row was well underway. The 1920s Art Deco shops on the left had replaced the last of the early nineteenth-century houses which graced the edge of the Calthorpe Estate. The widening of Islington Row into a dual carriageway was one of the first stages of what was to become the Middle Ring Road. An early JCB digger has been at work on the corner of Frederick Road. A Metro-Cammell-bodied Daimler 'Fleetline' CRG6LX, 3712 (KOX 712F), travels away from Five Ways when working on the Inner Circle route, followed by a Singer Chamois rear-engined saloon, which was an upmarket Hillman Imp. (Birmingham Public Works Dept)

Opposite: Islington Row. On the corner of Enfield Street and just above the entrance to Five Ways station, was the impressively-windowed Victorian premises of the City of Birmingham Welfare Department. This had originally been the site of Enfield Hall, but was replaced at the end of the nineteenth century by the Edgbaston Vestry Office which housed the parish records and in which the ratepayers met their councillors. The line of cars in Islington Row would make a modern-day car enthusiast's mouth water; a Ford Cortina 113E waits behind an Austin A35 van belonging to Silcox and Smith (who were electricians based at Hampstead Road), a Hillman Husky III, a Volkswagon Kombi van, and behind the Bradford's bread van, a rare Austin A70 Hampshire – a model only in production between 1949 and 1950.

The Anchor Inn on the corner of Islington Row and Tennant Street in 1957. Four years later the pub and the block of shops were gone. There had been an Anchor Inn in Islington Row since at least 1804. Kunzles, well remembered for their delicious cakes, are a couple of shops up from the Anchor.

One of the best-known shops and landmarks on the No. 8 route, the premises of Faulkes the furriers, Tudor House, at 47 to 49 Islington Row. The company was founded by a brother and sister George and Elizabeth Faulkes, shown below with their other brothers and fellow directors Richard and Charles. The company started in 1927 on the Alum Rock Road in Saltley , but soon moved to extended premises in Islington Row where it remained until 1963. Faulkes then moved virtually round the corner to Calthorpe Road until 1990.

The shop interiors were Aladdin's caves of antiques and stuffed animals and birds. Pictured here is the Chinese room, which had to be seen to be believed. It was described as 'having all the beauty and mystery of a scene from the Arabian nights'.

One of the Faulkes' craftsmen at work. When the company was founded in the 1920s there were thirty competitors in Birmingham, by the time of the move to Calthorpe Road there were just seven and now there are none or, at least, none who advertise.

FIVE WAYS STATION. B'HAM.

Five Ways Station on the Midland Railway's West Suburban line has had a chequered career. It opened after the other Midland Railway stations on 1 July 1885, replacing the station at Granville Street which was nearer the centre of Birmingham. The problem with Five Ways was the number of steps down from street level in Islington Row. Competition from bus services and the strictures of war resulted in the 'temporary' closure of the station on 2 October 1944, which became permanent in November 1950. For the next twenty-eight years the station was left to gently crumble away, only the waiting shelters and the platform flagstones were actually removed. Eventually, the rebuilt station was opened on 8 May 1978 when the cross-city line from Redditch to Four Oaks was introduced with funding from the local authorities, British Rail, Centro and West Midlands P.T.E. This pre-1914 view towards the tunnels which led to New Street Station shows the original brick arched bridge in Islington Row as well as the large Edgbaston Vestry Office on the left. (B. Geens Collection)

In their 1930s attempt to purchase buses from a second chassis manufacturer, Birmingham purchased five A.E.C. 'Regent' 0661s which had Wilson pre-select gearboxes. Numbered 1034-1038, they were fitted with M.C.C.W. bodies which looked very similar to the bodies supplied to the contemporary Daimler COG5s, except around the area below the windscreen. 1036 (CVP 136) entered service on 11 July 1937, just two months after the Leyland 'Titan' TD4c, with which they were in fuel competition. These buses were allocated to Liverpool Street garage and as a consequence they were regular performers on the Inner Circle route. Carrying an INNER CIRCLE radiator route slip-board, when new in 1937, A.E.C. 'Regent' 1036 has climbed past the three-storey terraces in Lee Bank Road and has just passed the entrance to Wheeleys Road. (J. Cull)

About twenty years later, in the same place as the previous photograph, is the last of the fifty Leyland-bodied Leyland 'Titan' PD2/1s, 2180 (JOJ 180). The bus driver pulls heavily on the steering wheel as he negotiates the small, but awkwardly-shaped, island at the junction with Wheeleys Road. Coming around the island and waiting for the bus to pass, is a Hillman Minx Series II, while following the speedy Leyland is a February 1953 registered Morris Oxford MO saloon, and an Austin K8 Three Way van which is passing a parked Fordson E83W 10cwt van. In the background to the right are the cramped pre-1850s courts of Lee Bank Road, while to the left of the corner shop are the even older three-storied back-to-back houses in Great Colmore Street. (A.B. Cross)

Numbers 52-53 Lee Bank Road, dating from the early ninteenth century, were the premises of Bruce Harris, electrical engineers, in 1948.

Lee Crescent in 1954 with a large 1948 Austin rivalling in elegance the Regency-style housing. The road was never on the No. 8 route but with the opening up of Lee Bank this street of listed buildings is very visible from the bus. Lee Crescent makes quite a contrast with the Lee Bank estate on the other side of the road.

Once the densely-packed and unhealthy back-to-backs on Lee Bank were demolished, the wide open green spaces seemed to emphasise the steepness of the important link between Five Ways and Bristol Street. The maisonettes at the bottom of the hill around Sun Street, with the multi-storey flats of Highgate in the distance, were part of the Lee Bank scheme that was designed by the then city architect, A.G. Sheppard Fidler, who had been appointed in 1952. The bus is pulling away from the stop near Lee Mount is a Daimler-engined Daimler 2718 (JOJ 718), with an M.C.C.W. H30/24R body. Dating from 1 September 1951, this bus was already about fifteen years old. (A.D. Broughall)

The 150-acre Central Redevelopment Area based on Lee Bank began in the early 1960s, with mid-Victorian terraces, courtyards and back-to-backs pulled down and replaced by multi-storey flats. There were four high-rise blocks between Lee Bank and Bell Barn Road. These buildings were very new when 'new-look' fronted Crossley DD42/7, 2441 (JOJ 441), came down Lee Bank (later called Middleway). The Crossley sails past the elderly lady standing at the bus stop outside gates to the 1960-built Lee Mason Secondary School, now the James Brindley School, as it is being used as a driver trainer. In Birmingham, buses being used thus were more usually known as 'learners'. New drivers were tested on Crossleys or Leylands. They had synchromesh gearboxes, allowing the trainee to acquire an 'all-types' bus driving licence. (R.F. Mack)

The maisonettes in Sun Street, with Spring Street in the background were part of the municipally-inspired Lee Bank Comprehensive Redevelopment scheme, designed to reduce the original population of 15,000 by just over half. The scheme began in 1952 but it was not until the late 1960s that the redevelopment was completed. By this time there were already concerns about the validity of multi-storey flats and municipally-owned inner city property when overspill areas such as Castle Vale and Bromford Bridge were using up much more attractively sited land at the edge of the city. Passing the entrance to Sun Street is 2789 (JOJ 789), a Liverpool Street garage-based Crossley-bodied Daimler CVG6 dating from 1 July 1952. It is travelling towards the junction with Bristol Street. (A.D. Broughall)

Waiting to cross Bristol Street from Sun Street into St Luke's Road is 1937-built Daimler COG5 1096 (CVP 196). This Metro-Cammell bodied bus is on an Inner Circle shortworking on 6 July 1959. 1096 was rebodied in February 1949 and remained in service until the end of May 1960. Behind the bus is a Daimler CVG6 of 1948. To the left, on the corner of Bristol Street is the Sun Inn, while on the right is Horace Baxter's boot and shoe repairers. (R.F. Mack)

The Inner Circle route crossed Bristol Street, from Sun Street into St Luke's Road, where the traffic lights are located on the right. Tram 512, the first of the United Electric Car Company-built eight-wheeled cars of 1913, loads two young ladies in summer frocks in exchange for several dour-looking men, when working into the city centre terminus in Navigation Street in 1951. Behind the tram is the Sun Inn. On the right is the Gothic-styled, but spireless St Luke's church built in 1902, replacing an earlier Victorian structure. The tram has come into town on the 72 route from Longbridge. Behind the Morris Eight is tram 772. This totally-enclosed tramcar, dating from 1928, had recently been transferred from working on the tram routes operated by Washwood Heath depot and is working on the 70 route to Rednal. (D.R. Harvey Collection)

The Bristol Road ABC, renamed as the Cinerama, in 1963. Around the corner from here at Christmas time in 1959 one of the city's most notorious crimes took place, the murder of Stephanie Baird, at the Edgbaston YWCA hostel. For some time the city was transfixed by the hunt for the prime suspect, a heavily bloodstained man who, on the night of the murder, had boarded the No. 8 at Bristol Road and travelled to Saltley.

This ABC was one of the more important cinemas in Birmingham, with its proximity to the city making it central rather than suburban. It opened on 16 May 1937 and survived until 24 September 1987 when it was closed and quickly demolished. Showing is the 1965 film *The Battle of the Bulge* as a new look front Crossley DD42/7 comes out of the newly cut, but unfinished Lee Bank. In the foreground is the abandoned Sun Street while traffic waiting to cross Bristol Road comes out of the section of Belgrave Road whose wide centre section was an underpass in waiting. Ottowa Tower, in the centre, stands above the nearby maisonettes and Belgrave Road police station. The lower blocks of flats, under construction on the right, were demolished in 2001. On the left are the remnants of 1840s houses on the corner of Pershore Road and Belgrave Road. (J. Moss)

Three
Belgrave Road to Stratford Road

Belgrave Road looking towards Balsall Heath and the Moseley Road, in an aerial view from 1987. Belgrave Road had, by this date, become the Belgrave Middleway and this view shows much of the Super Prix course. St Luke's church, Matthew Boulton College and the Central Mosque are to the left of the Middleway while to the right are Percy Shurmer School, the Birmingham Sports Centre and Joseph Chamberlain College.

The cab door of the fairly new 1870 (HOV 870), one of the hardworking Metro-Cammell bodied Daimler CVG6s, is open as the driver waits to 'peg' the Bundy Clock in the by now very run-down Sherlock Street. The bus still has the large fleet numbers on the rear panel which were starting to be replaced in 1953, when advertisements were placed roughly in the same place. It was Friday 7 December 1951, still in the days of the hand-pushed cart, two of which are standing in the road behind the bus. Parked facing the traffic lights on the right is a White's Bedford removal van registered in January 1948 with an HOX mark which was specifically reserved for commercial vehicles. (D.R. Harvey Collection)

1030 (CVP 130) turns from Sherlock Street into Belgrave Road, winter 1959. Behind the bus on the left is Caroline Villas, dating from 1839 and typical of the houses built in Balsall Heath at the time. This area's proximity to the Calthorpe Estate's protected middle-class development, meant that the Gouch family initially sold off land for better quality houses than the squalid terraces built after the Crimean War. This Metro-Cammell bodied Daimler COG5, had entered service on 1 August 1937 and in 1959 was a Highgate Road bus. By this time, the pre-war Daimlers were getting a bit old and although they enjoyed a revival between 1958 and the spring of 1960, they were usually only used on shortworkings – in hot weather they had a tendency to boil! 1030 went, in May 1960, along with most of the other Birmingham buses withdrawn at this time, to the 'Bardic' scrapman, W.T. Bird of Stratford-upon-Avon. (R.F. Mack)

Matthew Boulton College. The building on the corner of Sherlock Street and Belgrave Road was described as 'colourful and self cleaning'. The college has quite a history in terms of its name and location. It was first opened in 1895 in Suffolk Street in the city centre and was known as the Municipal College. In 1927 it became the Birmingham Technical College and in 1950 the College of Technology, Commerce and Art. It was rebuilt on its present site during 1966-68, on land bought from St Luke's church.

Having passed the checker-board frontage of the Matthew Boulton College, 2777 (JOJ 777), a Daimler CVG6 with a Crossley H30/25R body dating from July 152, speeds across the Varna Road junction whilst on the 8 route. It was travelling along a section of the road which had already had the old Victorian terraces demolished, leaving a wideopen space of waste ground which would become part of the Middleway's dual carriageway. Varna Road and the nearby Princess and Alexandra Roads were still hanging on to their dubious reputation of being in the 'red light' district of Birmingham, which would also be swept away when the once-elegant semi-detached villas on the Balsall Heath side were demolished (D.R. Harvey Collection).

2572 (JOJ 572), a Guy 'Arab' III Special, with a Metro-Cammell body, dating from 1 December 1950, barks its way along Belgrave Road heading towards Pershore Road. This bus was in 1968 operated by Liverpool Street garage, which belatedly put these buses on the Inner Circle for the first time. Just visible in the background is a bus working on the 48 service through the redevelopers' wasteland in Gooch Street. Following 2572 is a Ford Zephyr Mk IV which is attempting to overtake it. Travelling towards Gooch Street is a Post Office-owned Austin LD van. This area was renamed Highgate, though even the pleasant name could hardly mask the deterioration of the maisonettes. Today, these blocks have been extensively renovated and updated. (J.H. Taylforth Collection)

While the work on the Bristol Road and Pershore Road junctions was taking place, the line of the Inner Circle was frequently altered. On one such occasion, the 8 route was diverted alomg Gooch Street, although the line of the road was later to be changed to run in front of the first new shops to be built in Highgate after the redevelopment had begun. The bus is 2482, (JOJ 482), a Crossley DD42/7 with a Crossley body dating from August 1950. In front of the bus, in the centre of the road, is a patchwork of repaired road surface. This central strip was where the single tram track for the inbound 37 and 39 tram routes was situated, which had been abandoned in 1949! (J.H. Taylforth Collection)

It is hard to believe that nothing is left today of this 1960s scene and that this community was swept away as part of the dual carriageway of the Middleway. Wrenson's Stores stood on the corner of Longmore Street and Belgrave Road and was one of this Birmingham-based family grocer's many outlets in the city. This one had the telephone number CALthorpe 3649. On the opposite corner of Longmore Street was the long-forgotten Eagle Inn. Behind the Bournemouth-registered standard Eight dating from 1947 and the Bedford CA van is the Victorian terrace between Alexandra Road and Princess Road, while the larger houses with gabled attics are nearer Pershore Road. The bus is one of the first post-war Daimler CVG6s with Metro-Cammell bodies which were something of a rarity on the 8 service. 1592, (GOE 592), entered service on 1 January 1948 and would survive until the end of October 1966. (D.R. Harvey Collection)

The drop from Moseley Road down Belgrave Road to the Gooch Street junction was about 70ft, but actually looked a lot steeper from the top deck of an Inner Circle bus. The massive twenty-storey Binklow Tower block overlooks Belgrave Road, at a time when building high was perceived as the salvation for replacing the slums of inner cities such as those found in Birmingham. Today, the derelict land to the left of the the bus is the location of Birmingham's impressive Central Mosque. The bus is 2706 (JOJ 706), a Daimler-engined Daimler CVD6 with a Metro-Cammell body dating from 1 September 1951. (D.R. Harvey Collection)

Looking along Belgrave Road to the Central Mosque in 1976, just after the mosque opened. The mosque stands on the site of Dare's Brewery. Work started on the mosque in 1968 and it was completed in 1975. The landmark minaret was added in 1982 and is 150ft high. Inside there is room for 4,000 Muslims to pray. It also houses a library and community centre as well as acting as a mortuary.

A courtyard at the rear of 170 Belgrave Road, close to Dare's Brewery. The houses pictured here in June 1962 were soon to be demolished. These were the type of courtyards found along the length of Belgrave Road.

The No. 8 route turned into a motor racing circuit. This scene, at the top of Belgrave Middleway, shows a Formula Ford 1600 race, one of the supporting races to the main Formula 3000 Super Prix. This was the event's second year, in 1987. The races were held during August Bank holidays until 1990. Although hugely popular with enthusiasts they were viewed very differently by some residents and local MP Clare Short told Parliament the they were unprofitable, a waste of money and deeply unpopular with her constituents. At the time of writing in 2002 the course is still marked by the concrete kerbing on the island that carried the advertisements for the local Halfords company.

The Midland Railway bridge over Highgate Road was renewed with a girder construction in October 1909. The railway was opened by the Birmingham & Gloucester Railway on 17 December 1840 and the station on the left was the third one to be named Camp Hill. The station and 'the Camp Hill line' closed as a wartime economy measure on 27 January 1941 and passenger facilities were never reinstated. The bridge was 'plated' at 14' 3", but was about 6in higher. Birmingham's buses, with an average height of 14' 4½", came up the hill in Belgrave Road and swooped over Moseley Road, with the Midland Bank on one corner and the Belgrave public house on the other then, just as it looked as though the top deck was about to hit the steel girder bridge, the bus plunged into the damp gloom, stopping to pick up passengers. Just beyond the bridge are the shops leading to Kyrwick's Lane. (R.S. Carpenter Collection)

The battered black and yellow hashing of the bridge indicates several encounters with high vehicles, usually HGVs. Beneath it is a Mercedes-Benz 0405N, 1686 (T686 FOB). The bus is about to climb the short steep rise to cross Moseley Road and join the Middle Ring Road. Through the bridge are the wide open spaces created in Highgate Road when the Victorian terraces were demolished in the 1970s. This allowed the parallel side streets such as Ombersley Road, to 'breathe', making the formerly grim Highgate Road into a tree-lined routeway between Moseley Road and Ladypool Road. (D.R. Harvey)

In June 1947, the Inner Circle bus route was diverted away from Highgate Road because of road works. The buses were sent round the block, by way of Ladypool Road, Ombersley Road and Woodfield Road. 1210 (FOF 210), a Daimler COG5 with a Metro-Cammell H30/24R body waits to turn into Woodfield Road while an inspector gives the driver directions. The three-storied Victorian industrial building belonged to Charles Brecknell who manufactured weighing machines. To the right the small row of shops included a newsagents, grocers and a drapers shop on the corner of Woodfield Road. Beyond the bus is the Camp Hill railway line bridge with the south end Camp Hill Railway Station just to the right of the double set of signals. Bus 1210 was to become well known after its sale in 1954 as it worked with Clyde Coast Services of Ardrossan, until December 1962. (A.N.H. Glover)

Urban blight in Highgate Road in 1977. These properties were about to be swept away. Shown here are Olive's Cafe, 'Mrs Olive Fleming's Dining rooms' according to Kelly's Directory, and Highgate TV Service, with the Wild's Buildings between the two.

Travelling along Highgate Road, having left the distant and by now closed Highgate Road garage behind 1872 (HOV 872), a Metro-Cammell-bodied Daimler CVG6 passes the patched-up and soon to be demolished Victorian terraces on its way towards Moseley Road. Bus 1872 was for many years based at Highgate Road garage, but when that garage closed on 14 July 1962, the bus was transferred to Liverpool Street garage, continuing much as before working on its old haunts on the Inner Circle until its withdrawal in early 1968. (R.F. Mack)

One of the worst bombing raids of the Second World War occurred on the night of 19 November 1940. It was on this night that Highgate Road bus garage was bombed, causing considerable damage to the Queen Street side of the garage and the houses opposite the side of the garage. Bus 814 (BOP 814), was parked in Queen Street and was completely blown over by the blast. It is seen here lying on its side on the following morning. The Birmingham Railway Carriage & Wagon-built body was badly damaged and was replaced on 1 January 1942 by a streamlined body which had been intended for a Manchester Corporation bus, whose chassis had been destroyed in the infamous bombing of Coventry, also in November 1940. What is perhaps surprising is that this damaged body was in use again by March 1941 on another Daimler, 901 (COH 901). (D.R. Harvey Collection)

The Queen's Arms in 2002, owned and run for the last fifteen years by Tommy and Phyllis. The pub once boasted its own brewery and the old brew house still stands at the rear of the premises.

Approaching the old Brewers' Arms, in Highgate Road is Mercedes-Benz 0405N, 1681 (T681 FOB). It is working on the 8A service on 25 May 2002. Despite its size, at 12m long, these buses, with their long front and rear overhangs, have a seating capacity for only forty-three passengers, eleven less than the pre-war Daimler COG5s and Leyland TD6cs which used to slog their way around the Inner Circle in the years immediately before, during and after the war. To the left, the bus passes The Queen's Arms public house, which stands on the opposite corner to the former Highgate Road bus garage. (D.R. Harvey)

The New "Brewers' Arms,"

—— HIGHGATE ROAD, ——
SPARKBROOK, BIRMINGHAM.

Proprietors:
MESSRS. SHOWELLS' BREWERY CO. LTD.,
Langley, Birmingham.

Architect:
W. NORMAN TWIST, ESQ., F.R.I.B.A.,
Queen's College, Paradise Street, Birmingham.

Builders:
MESSRS. C. BRYANT & SON, LTD.,
Whitmore Road, Small Heath, Birmingham.

The new Brewers' Arms, pictured in a programme for its opening after refurbishment on 15 September 1927. The evening featured a 'Grand Concert' in The Assembly Room. The owners had 'endeavoured to provide an ideal inn of moderate size embodying the latest ideas in hygienic construction whilst still retaining the pleasing features of the old half-timbered English inn.'

The last exposed-radiator bus to be delivered to B.C.T. was 2425 (JOJ 425). It entered service on 1 June 1950 and was a Crossley DD42/7 with a Crossley downdraught HOE7/5B 8.6 litre engine and a heavyweight Crossley H30/24R body. Crossleys had manual synchromesh gearboxes, which were easier to manage than other manufacturers' gearboxes. Around 1958, the crew of the bus are waiting at the Bundy Clock outside the half-timbered Brewers' Arms for their departure time, while the passengers sitting in the bus wonder when their journey will be renewed. (R.F. Mack) Today, this pub has been transformed into a Balti restaurant, the Lahore Karahi (below). (Barbara Palmer).

Four
Sparkbrook to Aston Cross

The corner of Medlicott and Walford Roads. The clock on Wainwright's automobile electricians shows ten past three and the date is 21 May 1964. Walford Road still has a number of the old-fashioned corner shops that were so much a part of the No. 8 route.

The advertisement on the side of the bus for 'Los Angeles. Non-stop Daily', could also have been the proclamation for the Inner Circle bus route, as it seemingly went on from early morning darkness, with the dawn chorus of factory shift workers, through to the last of the evening revellers staggering home on a Saturday night. 2726 (JOJ 726), one of the 1952 batch of Daimler CVD6s, crosses Stratford Road into Highgate Road from Walford Road although its destination number blind has slipped. The bus is nearly full up with passengers on this hot summer's day explaining why all the saloon ventilators are open. (C. Carter)

The suburb of Sparkbrook was developed from the late 1840s on land near the Angel pub at the junction of Ladypool Road and Stratford Road. The land of the former Mole Estate contained many back-to-back houses, but by the end of the 1890s the area around the Stoney Lane junction had been built up with mainly the later tunnel-back terraces as well as the larger villas and gabled shops along Stratford Road. Until the mid-1960s the layout of the Stratford Road junction at Stoney Lane in Sparkbrook, meant that the Inner Circle came out of Walford Road, which is just beyond the double-decker on the left, and turned into Stratford Road to briefly face the city centre. The Midland Red B.M.M.O. S13 single-decker is at the point where the 8 route turned left into Stoney Lane where one of Yardley Wood garage's Daimler CVD6s is turning when working on the 13 service. The Inner Circle then turned right into Highgate Road before arriving at the corporation bus garage. (D.R. Harvey Collection)

Towards the end of the B.C.T. era, a number of the new-look-front buses were fitted with a plain wire mesh grill in place of the original chromed slotted radiator cover. Coupled with the front wings being cut back by about six inches in order that the brakes had a better flow of cooling air over them, by the late 1960s the smart frontal appearance of many buses in the Birmingham fleet took on a 'home-made look' as exemplified here by Daimler CVD6 2704 (JOJ 704), a Metro-Cammell-bodied fifty-four seater which dated from September 1951. It would be withdrawn at the end of October 1969, just one month after acquisition by West Midlands P.T.E. 2704 is halfway across Stratford Road having exited Walford Road with the recently closed Midlands Electricity Board showroom on the left. Between the back of the bus and the following 1961 Smethwick registered Ford Anglia 105E deluxe, is the advertising hoarding on the forecourt of the Waldorf Cinema. This picture house operated from 1913 until 1981. Despite having an 820-seater auditorium, the Waldorf was always the poor relation of the nearby Piccadilly in Stratford Road. The Waldorf was never part of any of the main cinema chains and as a consequence never seemed to get anything other than very old feature films or very 'B' second features. As if to prove the point, in this 1968 scene, the film showing is Ivanhoe starring Robert Taylor which dated from 1952. Next door to the cinema is the quaint, brick-built snooker and billiards hall, which survives today, and beyond that are the twin entrance towers of the Embassy Sports Drome. (R.F. Mack)

Sid Field, famous Birmingham comedian. He is included here because of his connections with
the Waldorf Cinema. Born in 1904, as a child Sid Field lived nearby at 152 Osborn Road,
Sparkbrook and he first showed signs of his comic genius busking for the cinema crowds waiting
to go into the Waldorf. The cinema itself opened in 1913 as the Waldorf Picture Theatre. It
closed in 1981 and is now used as an Asian religious centre. Sid Field hit the big time just after
the end of the Second World War, but his success was cruelly cut short by his premature death
in 1950, when he was at the height of his fame.

Zetters Bingo Hall in Walford Road, previously the Embassy Sports Drome, May 1976.

On Saturday 7 February 1970, just five months after West Midlands P.T.E. had taken over from B.C.T., a Gardner 10.45 litre engined Daimler 'Fleetline CRG6LX, 3364 (364 KOV), a Metro-Cammell-bodied seventy-six seater dating from June 1964, speeds along Walford Road. These were among the first of the 1960s generation of rear-engined buses and were allocated to operate from Liverpool Street garage. Behind the bus is the Embassy Sports Drome, which was a roller skating rink but also staged ice-dance shows such as 'White Horse Inn on Ice' and regular boxing promotions, including the mid-1960s fights of the British Empire Heavyweight Champion, Johnny Prescott. Today, the site is a small estate of modern houses. The terraced houses on the right in Walford Road date from the 1890s and were built on the ill-drained land on the now culverted Spark Brook. (J. Carroll)

Probably the largest factory on the Inner Circle bus route was the Birmingham Small Arms complex in Armoury Road, although part of the factory faced Golden Hillock Road. Despite the horrendous bombing of the new building on 19 November 1940 which claimed the lives of fifty-three workers, the factory was back in full production soon afterwards. B.S.A. was started in 1861 by twelve local gun makers on a greenfield site between the Warwick and Birmingham and the Great Western Railway, but by 1889 the company were beginning to make bicycles in an attempt to diversify. Motorcycles first appeared in 1910, while three-wheeled cars were sporadically made from 1908 until 1930. The company took over Daimler in 1910 and from 1931, after Lanchesters were bought, until the outbreak of the Second World War, produced the smaller cars in B.S.A. group, with the 10hp and the Scout being the most popular models. The company went back to its armament routes during the Second World War, employing over 20,000 workers at twenty or so plants producing rifles, shells, bicycles and machine tools. During the hostilities B.S.A. manufactured 126,354 of their 496cc single cylinder motorcycles for the Allied forces. By February 1950, the Armoury Road factory was employing 3,500 workers making motorcycles. Parked in Armoury Road is a March 1937 registered Lanchester Eleven saloon. Unfortunately, this once mighty B.S.A. factory officially closed on 15 December 1975 and was demolished a few years later. (Birmingham City Engineers and Surveyors Dept)

To the north of the B.S.A. factory, on the Inner Circle bus route was a Great Western Railway station. The G.W.R. opened their station at Small Heath and Sparkbrook in April 1863, though it appears to have had a crisis of identity, being renamed Smallheath & Sparkbrook in April 1865 and then back again to its original name in January 1899. For the first four years of its existence, the main line from Birmingham Snow Hill to Paddington in London was dual gauge with the broad gauge tracks surviving until 1868. The entrance, booking hall and steps down to the platforms were built at a slight angle on Golden Hillock Road, which allowed for a small carriage waiting area, on the extreme left. In the early years of the British Railways, when the advertisement on the right shows that it cost 18/6d for a day excursion to Weston-Super-Mare, the word 'Great' had been painted over, shabbily removing the idea of 'God's Wonderful Railway' in favour of the Labour Government's Nationalisation programme. (Birmingham Central Reference Library)

Standing in the melting snow in February 1962 at the entrance to Midland Motors is a strange looking half-cab six-wheeled lorry. Painted in B.C.T. dark blue and cream, this A.E.C. 'Renown' 663 model, had originally been a demonstrator to the corporation, being registered in Middlesex in October 1931 as MV 489. Fitted with a Short Brothers H33/25R body, it was numbered 92 in the fleet, but only lasted until July 1937 when it was withdrawn and converted into this breakdown lorry. With the vestiges of its original lower saloon remaining, Service Vehicle 15, as it had become, was nicknamed 'The Ambulance', serving in this capacity until September 1961 when it was sold to Midland Motors of 149A Golden Hillock Road.

Victoria Park after the devastating tornado which spectacularly hit Small Heath on 12 June 1931.

This is the important six-way junction in Golden Hillock Road, with Cooksey Road and Glover Road to the left and Wordsworth Road and Waverley Road to the right. The awkwardly shaped traffic island was always a trial of strength for drivers on the Inner Circle coming from Coventry Road, as they almost had to turn into the entrance to Small Heath Park. The 41 1/2 acre park had been presented 'as a noble gift' to Birmingham corporation by Louisa Anne Ryland and was opened to the public on 5 April 1878. It was renamed in 1887 when the Queen paid a visit as part of her Golden Jubilee celebrations. Dominating the junction was the Co-operative at number 72. This was branch number 33 and combined, oddly, a butcher's and dry cleaner's. On Friday 21 March 1958, although there is not a bus in sight, there are a number of people waiting at the bus stop. (Birmingham City Engineers & Surveyors Dept)

The Inner Circle route crossed Coventry Road by taking left turns out of Golden Hillock Road
(on the left) and Muntz Street on the right, and then right turns into each of these roads. A
one-ton van and a cyclist wait in the centre of Coventry Road for the procession of limousines
and the 1928 Brush-bodied Midland Red SOS QL to pass into the city centre. Some of the large
houses on the left, between Golden Hillock Road and Langley Road, which dated from the
1860s, had already been converted to shops in this 1934 view. Careful inspection of the
overhead wires spanning the road reveals that the trolleybuses have taken over from the trams.
The two Corporation buses in this view are of types which were rarely pictured. Coming out of
Golden Hillock Road is an open-staircase 'pick-pocket special' dating from 1928. This is an
A.D.C. 507 with a Short lowbridge body and it is working towards Saltley. The vehicle working
on the outer, clockwise Inner Circle was unique in Birmingham. The bus is 99 (OF 3959),
which was the Corporation's only Leyland 'Titan' TD1. It had a Leyland L24/24R body which
made it ideal to work under the low bridges in Highgate Road and Icknield Street and was one
of the first buses in the Birmingham fleet to receive what was called at the time an oil engine.
(J. Whybrow Collection)

Turning out of Muntz Street into Coventry Road in May 1970 is a two-and-a-half-year-old Daimler 'Fleetline' CRG6LX. 3699 (KOX 699F), bodied by Metro-Cammell-Weymann was a bit heavy to drive in the days before power steering and turns like this demanded a sound driving technique from the man behind the steering wheel, who in this case looks remarkably unflustered. The public house on the corner of Muntz Street is the Malt Shovel, the exterior of which has survived to the present day remarkably unaltered. (D.R. Harvey Collection)

All the properties between Coventry Road and Wright Street have survived, though the Methodist church dating from 1870, next to which the Austin Cambridge A55 is parked, was swept away with the houses on the left in the 1980s. The shop passed by the young man on the right was an off-licence, which might have led to an uncomfortable juxtaposition with the teetotal Methodists across the road! Travelling along Muntz Street towards Coventry Road is exposed-radiatored Daimler CVG6, 1861 (HOV 861), which although about sixteen years old was still reliably pounding the Inner Circle service and would be used in all-day duty on this and other routes operated by Liverpool Street garage until the end of February 1968. (R.F. Mack)

With only one stop between Green Lane and Coventry Road and a slight descent around the curve into Muntz Street, this was a section of the route where the drivers could 'put their foot down' and perhaps gain a little time. This is what the driver of Crossley-bodied Daimler CVG6 2792 (JOJ 792), appears to be doing as he speeds past Somerville Road and its little grocer's shop on the corner. On the distant corner of Muntz Street were the premises of J.E. House & Son, bakers. In the late 1950s they bucked the trend for steam baked bread and made superb cottage loafs, batches and bloomers, as well as the most magnificent dripping cakes imaginable. (R.F. Mack)

Crossing the Green Lane junction with Victoria Street is a 1963 Daimler 'Fleetline' CRG6LX, 3327 (327 GON). Travelling towards Bordesley Green is a Ford Cortina Mk II. The bus is approaching the fare stage at The Vine public house, which stands between Green Lane – where The Candy Shop, on the extreme right, is situated – and Grange Road. These flat-fronted Metro-Cammell-Weymann-bodied rear-engined buses, with their comparatively lightweight body structures, lasted a lot longer in service than originally envisaged. For instance, 3327, by now running for the still fairly recently formed W.M.P.T.E., lasted until the end of January 1979. (Travel Lens)

In about 1965, 2460 (JOJ 460), a Crossley-bodied Crossley DD42/7 of 1950 stands waiting for the traffic lights to change before crossing from Bordesley Green Road into Victoria Street. It has climbed the long 'drag' from Adderley Park Station with a full load of Inner Circle passengers. Coming out of Cherrywood Road alongside the impressive Victorian two-storey Barclays Bank building, is an Austin Minivan, while behind the Crossley is another product of Longbridge, an Austin Cambridge A60. Behind the bus, to the right, are the early postwar premises of Matthews & Wilson, manufacturing joiners. (R.F. Mack)

To anyone in Birmingham who owned an old car from the 1950s until the 1980s, Meadway Spares, in Bordesley Green Road, was almost certainly well known. Here one could find almost any spare engine or body part for almost any make of car. The barracks-like building was the old Civic Restaurant, while in front of the building's entrance is one of those chilling road safety notices which were updated every month to show how many people were killed and injured on the roads of the city. Coming up the hill from Adderley Park railway station on 19 May 1955 is 1846, one of the ubiquitous HOV-registered Gardner 6LW engined Daimlers. (D.R. Harvey Collection)

Above: Looking up the hill towards Bordesley Green on 23 February 1956, the Thornley &
Knight paint factory is on the left, the northern edge of the Meadway Spares scrapyard on the
right and the northern limit of Victorian residential growth in Bordesley Green Road. One of
the paint manufacturers in Bordesley Green Road could well have supplied the paint and
varnish which adorned the body panels of the corporation's fleet of buses. On the left is
Burbidge Road, next to which was another paint manufacturer, Arthur Holden, and beyond
that was Mulliners, the well-known vehicle bodybuilder who for many years specialized in
military buses for the British armed forces. (Birmingham Central Reference Library)

St Saviour's Church was built in 1849 at the top of Ash Road, so that it might be visible from both Saltley to the north and Bordesley to the south. This large church was designed by R.C. Hussey in the Gothic Perpendicular style, but work was suspended for many years due to the parish running out of money. An imposing spire was added to the tower in 1871, but had to be removed when it fell into disrepair. This view of the church is from Ash Road, along which the Inner Circle begins its descent into valley of the River Rea. On the left is Hall Road and beyond are the Victorian houses in St Saviour's Road. (Commercial postcard)

Left: Adderley Park station was opened by the London & North Western Railway on 1 August 1860 on their main line to London. When it opened, it was located in what was then almost countryside on the east side of Bordesley Green Road, with only the nearby St Peter's College, begun in 1847 and completed in 1849 as a training establishment for male teachers, for company. Through the smoke is the Station Hotel on the city side of the same road, situated almost next to the Morris-Commercial van and lorry factory. Thundering through Adderley Park Station, with the station names on its gas lights, is a Birmingham to London Euston express train. The train's locomotive is 5902, named 'Sir Frank Ree', one of the two prototype 'Patriot' Class 5XP 4-6-0s, which were built in 1930 using parts from former L.N.W.R. Claughton-type locomotive. It is seen in its original condition, in about 1932, without smoke deflectors and would last in this condition until 1961. (R.S. Carpenter Collection)

In the gardens behind the Victorian terraced houses in Ash Road, which dated from the turn of the 1870s, were the remains of Saltley Hall, parts of which dated from the seventeenth century. This had been built by the Adderley family, on the site of the medieval Saltley manor house, and was abandoned by them when they began to industrialize the rural area of Saltley in the late 1840s. By 1970, all that remained of the Adderley family seat was some hummocky ground, which is seen next to and in front of the greenhouse, marking the site of the old buildings that had played such an important part of the 'manor' for over 700 years. (D.R. Harvey)

At the bottom of Ash Road the buses turned right at the Addeley Park Inn into Adderley Road, passing a number of factories, including Wilkinson's rolled steel works. The road was named after the Adderley family, landowners in the Saltley area since 1640. Charles Adderley financed the building of houses in the area from 1855. He had repeatedly complained about 'the pestilential stench' coming from the River Tame – the recipient of all Birmingham's sewage. Despite building the town's first sewage farm in 1865, the rapid growth of the town led to Saltley becoming 'a sodden morass'. However, due to the efforts of Adderley and Joseph Chamberlain, plans for sewage farms and filtration beds finally reached fruition in the 1880s, allowing Saltley to revert to a fresh-smelling suburb – except for the smell from the recently constructed gas works! 1925 (HOV 925), a M.C.C.W.-bodied Daimler CVG6 travels along Adderley Road towards The Gate at Saltley during 1963. (A. Yates)

Waiting at the Bundy Clock in Adderley Road in front of the late-1850s heavily pedimented houses, is one of Barford Street garage's buses, pictured between June 1953 (when small Coronation flag clips were fitted to all the postwar bus fleet) and April 1954 (when Barford Street garage closed). These houses were regarded when built as superior artisans through terraces. 1621 (GOE 621), a Metro-Cammell-bodied bus entered service on 1 February 1948 and would remain in service until 31 October 1966. (D.R. Harvey Collection)

The Gate, Saltley, was an Atkinson's Brewery-owned public house at the junction of Alum Rock Road and Adderley Road on the site of an eighteenth-century toll gate. Opposite was High Street and Washwood Heath Road. Turning into Adderley Road from High Street is one of the short length Guy 'Arab' III Specials. It is 29 September 1969, which was the penultimate day of B.C.T.'s operations before giving way to the new area operator, West Midlands P.T.E., a result of Barbara Castle's Transport Act of 1968. With their soft suspension it is surprising that 2566 (JOJ 566) isn't heeling over more as the driver accelerates towards his well-earned break at the Bundy Clock. Waiting at the traffic lights is an A.E.C. Marshall six-wheeled tipper fitted with a Leyland-designed 'Ergomatic' cab. (A. Yates)

The junction in Saltley has always had a particular place in the hearts of Brummies, seemingly because of it being the first crossroads 'over the river' from Birmingham. Saltley had been developed from the early 1840s on land owned by Charles Adderley and rapidly changed from a rural, willow-wooded area into an industrial urban landscape. It was incorporated into Birmingham in 1891, by which time The Gate area was virtually complete. All that remains of the old buildings are those lining Alum Rock Road, to the right and the few earlier nineteenth-century houses on the south side of Washwood Heath Road. (Barbara Palmer)

Right: Tuesday 1 August 1967. The trams and the tram tracks have long since disappeared and Ford Anglias and Hillman Minxes have replaced pre-war Morris Eights and Austin Tens. 2783 (JOJ 783), a Crossley-bodied Daimler CVG6, travels along High Street, Saltley, followed by an Austin Series 3 5-tonner lorry. On the right is the fairly recently opened café, while opposite are the shops of Phillip Collier, Edward's undertakers and the distant Midland Bank on the corner of Hereford Square. (A. Yates)

Above: There is not much evidence in this photograph of the 'clearing in the willows', which is what Saltley originally meant. The last of the medieval open-field systems had been enclosed in 1817 and the land owned by the Adderley family between the newly-built railway crossing and the old toll junction was rapidly developed from the 1850s onwards. In 1950 Saltley was still a prosperous Victorian shopping centre. A Fordson E83W 10cwt bread van turns into High Street passing Morrells wine merchants and the double-fronted tailor's shop of J.H. Bentley as it follows a very elderly two-door car. Passing through High Street are two 1928-built air-braked Brush totally-enclosed 63hp trams. Car 792 is coming towards The Gate while 770 works towards the city along High Street. (R.T. Wilson)

The climb from High Street over Saltley Viaduct began at Crawford Street, left. Saltley Viaduct opened in May 1895, replacing a level crossing on the Midland Railway. The Inner Circle service shared the road with the Washwood Heath (10) and Alum Rock (8) trams as well as the buses travelling to Glebe Farm on the 14 route. Tram 780 is travelling towards The Gate while the brand-new Crossley DD42/7, 2400 (JOJ 400), is working into the city. Towering over the industrialized River Tame valley are the gas holders in Nechells Place. The aroma from the coal gas production plants was a noxious reminder of the main industry of the area. (R.T. Wilson)

Having just passed the bricked-up entrance to the long-closed Saltley station, an air-brake Brush-built tram 779 of 1928, fitted with a pantograph, rumbles down Saltley Viaduct on its way to The Gate junction in the summer of 1950. On the left is the headquarters and works of Metropolitan-Cammell, who built many of Birmingham's bus bodies. In the distance, at the far end of the narrow High Street shopping area, a Daimler COG5 is turning out of Adderley Road on the inner ring working of the Inner Circle. (F. Lloyd Jones)

Saltley Railway Station was opened by Midland Railway on 1 October 1854 just to the north of Saltley Road. It was part of the MR's route to Burton-upon-Trent and Derby. The main island platform was reached from an entrance on the viaduct by way of the roofed stairs, visible on the left. On the island platform were the usual collection of waiting rooms, toilets and baggage rooms. It is seen on 27 May 1929, by which time it was under the ownership of the L.M.S. Railway. Saltley station closed on 4 March 1968 along with other stations on the line such as Bromford Bridge. (R.S. Carpenter Collection)

As Brush-built, totally-enclosed tramcar 770, built in 1928, waits in Saltley Road before moving off over Saltley Viaduct, one of Rosebery Street garage's Leyland-bodied Leyland 'Titan' TD6cs turns into Nechells Place, working on the Inner Circle bus route in 1950. The large building just to the left of the bus is the West Midlands Gas Board's main production centre whose yard always seemed full of coke. In the triangle on which the decanted tram passengers stand is a strange mixture of urban street furniture, with a telephone box, a brick-built urinal and a horse trough in evidence. (R.T. Wilson)

Towards the end of B.C.T. operation, the buses which began to encroach onto the 8 route were of types not used before. The final withdrawal of the exposed-radiator HOV-registered Daimler CVG6s in 1968 meant that as new buses were introduced on other services, the rear entrance, open-back platform bus was still considered the ideal vehicle in the days when passengers thought nothing of jumping on and off a moving bus. 3013 (MOF 13), a Guy 'Arab' IV with a fifty-five seater Metro-Cammell body, which first entered service in July 1953 as part of the final tram replacement fleet, begins to pull out of Nechells Place on its way towards Saltley Viaduct, displaying a 'lazy' destination blind. (R.F. Mack)

Looking down Nechells Place towards Saltley Road, the West Midlands Gas Board gasometer towers over the battered mid-1850s terraced houses. On the right is Cato Street North with the Butlers Brewery-owned Albion Vaults public house occupying the angled corner site. The pub survives today, but everything else around it has long since been demolished. Metro-Cammell bodied Daimler CVG6, 1925 (HOV 925), climbs the steep hill travelling towards Nechells Green in about 1966, followed by a Commer Superpoise 30cwt van. It was always said that people who lived within the smell of Saltley's gas works, in the days when it was produced by using coal, would never catch a cold! (D.R. Harvey Collection)

A Morris Oxford MO crosses Nechells Green and an Inner Circle bus stands in Rocky Lane. Just in front of it is another Inner Circle bus, which validates the old theory of 'none for hours and then two turn up at once'! The bus is 1880 (HOV 880), an exposed-radiator Daimler CVG6 which is working towards Aston Cross. The bus in front is about to pass the Victorian terraces near Scholfield Street. This 1955 scene shows the area before it became one of the five Central Redevelopment Areas. On the right, belonging to the days before the MOT tests, is the Villa Service Station, which has for sale an early post-war Hillman Minx Phase I and a 1939 Ford Tudor 7Y saloon. (D.R. Harvey Collection)

One of the first tower blocks to be built after the demolition of the Victorian terraces was Camrose Tower. This eight-storey block was built on the corner of Cromwell Street and Rocky Lane. With Nechells Place and the nearby gasworks just visible, 3173 (MOF 173), a 'new-look' front Daimler CVG6 with a Crossley H30/25R body which entered service on 25 March 1954, pulls away from the stop alongside the waste ground where once stood rows of terraces and squalid back-to-back courtyards. Behind is another of the HOV-registered Daimler CVG6s of 1949. (A.B. Cross)

The Inner Circle serves the entertainment complex at Star City only after 7 p.m. during week days, but has a regular all-day Sunday service. The Star City area was developed by the Richardson Brothers, who had been responsible for the construction of the hugely successful Merry Hill Centre at Brierley Hill in the Black Country. Using the old gas works as a basis for the design, Star City boasts cinemas and fast food outlets in an 'out of town' environment. (Barbara Palmer)

The railway bridge in Rocky Lane carried the former L.N.W.R. goods branch into Windsor Street Wharf, which originally opened in 1880, and the nearby Windsor Street gasworks which was the corporation's main gas producing works. Coal trains arrived almost hourly from the East Midlands coalfields and the line was electrified in 1967. However, after the introduction of natural gas from the North Sea, traffic declined, the gasworks closed and the railway line shut in 1980. The bridge was 15' 6" high and as a result, there was never any problem about getting double-deckers underneath it as Daimler CVG6 1920 (HOV 920) comfortably demonstrates, as it begins the climb to Nechells Green. (D.R. Harvey Collection)

Deep shadows cast on the rows of Victorian terraced houses by the factories lining Rocky Lane reflect the mix of industrial and residential landscapes that characterized so much of the Inner Circle bus route. Looking towards Aston Cross, the large factories on the right belong to C.A. Industrial Tubes, whose Climax Works have the wrought-iron entrance gates. Beyond them are the tall Britannia Works of the Hercules Cycle and Motor Company (shared with the James Cycle Company). The Hercules company formed in July 1919 and was part of the Tube Investment Group. Previously these premises accommodated the Dunlop Rubber Company. In the distance, opposite the chimney of the H.P. Sauce factory, are two buses working on the Inner Circle. Travelling towards Saltley is a HOV-registered Daimler CVG6, while on the left is the rear end of a Leyland-bodied Leyland PD2/1 from the 2131-2180 class of 1949-built buses. (D.R. Harvey)

Approaching Aston Cross from Rocky Lane, April 2002. The H.P. Sauce factory dominates both the skyline and the atmosphere of the junction. The distinctive dark brown sauce was first produced at Aston Cross in 1903. The H.P. name derived from the early popularity of the sauce in the House of Commons (Houses of Parliament) kitchens. (Barbara Palmer)

The last morning of tramcar operation in Birmingham was Saturday 4 July 1953. It continued like any other day until mid-morning, when replacement buses began to take over from the trams at Victoria Road. Sometime earlier car 620, a Brush-built, totally enclosed eight wheeler which dated from 1921, stands at Aston Cross, just short of the famous clock and Ansells Brewery. Coming out of Rocky Lane to the left of the Bedford O-type tipper lorry, is a Daimler CVG6 with a Crossley body which belonged to the buses numbered 2776-2900. It will cross the busy Victorian intersection and go straight across the junction alongside the Boots the chemist, just visible behind the traffic bollards, and pass into Park Lane. (A. Yates)

The Co-op shops, branch 43, at 6-16 Park Lane, Aston Cross. Park Road originally ran all the way from Aston Cross to Witton Lane but with the redevelopment of the Ansells brewery site it is now just an industrial cul-de-sac. The Co-op and other shops in the same block, such as Thompson's the butchers, reflected the real sense of community which was Aston Cross. The Co-op first started trading here in the late 1920s and was closed in the early 1970s.

A familiar view of Aston Cross in 1973. Nearly all of the street furniture in front of the 65 bus – a Park Royal-bodied Daimler 'Fleetline' – and the shops to the right have disappeared in recent times. The clock, however, remains, though it was moved a short distance down the road.

This scene at Aston Cross looking towards Lichfield Road hadn't altered for years, but everything was soon to change. In May 1953, 659, a locally-built M.R.C.W. totally-enclosed 40 hp tram headed towards the city on a 78 service while a similar-looking Brush-built tram of 1925, 696, worked on the 79 route to Pype Hayes. These thirty-year-old trams had only another two months to run. The famous Aston Cross clock was erected in 1881 to replace a much more ornate mock-Jacobean structure and still survives at Aston Cross, although in a slightly different location. The 1930s Ansells Brewery building was built on the site of a Georgian public house, but was itself to close in 1981 after an acrimonious industrial dispute. (A.N.H. Glover)

Aston Cross Picture House, a short distance off the route, was on Lichfield Road at the corner with Catherine Street. At one time there were two cinemas close to Aston Cross on the Lichfield Road, the Theatre Royal being the other. The Aston Cross Picture House opened in May 1913 with a seating capacity of 900. Designed, like the Bristol Road ABC, by Archibald Robinson, it also became an ABC cinema, changing its name to the ABC Aston in the fifties. It closed on 23 August 1969 and, after a short life as an Asian cinema, was demolished.

Aston Cross branch library, during renovation work in 1953. The library is one of the few surviving buildings from the old Aston Manor borough. It opened its doors on 30 October 1903. The library was a Carnegie building paid for by the Canadian philanthropist Andrew Carnegie and the site was the gift of the Ansells family. As a result of declining use in recent years the building is no longer a library but is used for student accommodation.

A very different view of the H.P. Sauce works, in December 1969, showing the construction of the Aston Expressway. The Expressway was built to ease traffic congestion along the Lichfield Road in and out of the city centre. It celebrates its thirtieth anniversary in 2002. The Expressway crosses the 8 route under Park Lane. It must be the only motorway in the country to be crossed by a vinegar main. The main, part of the H.P. works, was laid underground in 1906 but now has its own footbridge over the Expressway.

Five

Park Lane to Hockley Brook

Climbing Park Lane, Aston, is a bus working the Inner Circle route, c. 1937. The bus is 380 (OG 380), a 7.4 litre petrol-engined A.E.C. 'Regent' 661 with an English Electric forty-eight seater body. The bus entered service in September 1930 and would survive until July 1945, despite the somewhat bulbous lower saloon nearside panels, suggesting that all was not well with the body frame. Following the bus is a Morris Ten-Four of 1936. On the corner of Potters Hill is the butcher's shop belonging to H. Millington selling British meat at between 3d and 1s, albeit from unrefrigerated counters. Outside the shop, no doubt a boon to passing trade, is another bus stop bearing the legend 'Buses Stop Here By Request'. (Birmingham Central Reference Library)

The Eagle pub on the corner of Upper Sutton Street and Park Lane, September 1969. The pub, inevitably considering it was an Ansells inn, has long since disappeared.

Dropping off passengers in High Street, near Six Ways, Aston, is tramcar 581. The road to the left is Park Lane where the Inner Circle bus arrived at the top of Newtown from Aston Cross. The tram body was built by the United Electric Car Company on Mountain & Gibson Burnley Maximum traction bogies and entered service in February 1914. Car 581 was the first of four trams to be fitted out with curtains, cushions and carpets for the unsuccessful First Class service along Hagley Road – it lasted three months. Originally built with 40hp motors and open balconies, 581 lasted until the closure of the Birmingham tram system, by which time it had a 63hp motor was in this totally enclosed condition, which rather belied the mileage of over one million miles in thirty-nine years. (R.T. Wilson)

To the south of the Inner Circle bus route was the important Victorian suburb of Newtown, Aston UDC. Car 19, one of Birmingham Corporation's first tramcars, introduced on the service from Steelhouse Lane to Aston Brook on 4 January 1904, worked the route to Perry Barr. It would climb the hill to the left of the Barton's Arms and reach the point where the future Inner Circle bus route would cross its path at Park Lane. This tram route began on 1 January 1907, but only reached Perry Barr on 8 December 1908 after problems with running through what was then part of Handsworth UDC. The Barton's Arms was built in the last two years of the Victorian era, costing the brewery, Mitchells & Butlers some £22,000 to construct. Designed by Mr Brassington of James and Lister Lea, nothing was spared on the exterior, while the stunning Minton interior tilework, ornate woodwork, snob screens and stained glass were scarcely less lavish. It was threatened with demolition in 1969, but was happily reprieved and refurbished and survives today. On the right, on the corner of Newtown Row and Potter's Lane is the Aston Hippodrome. Opened on 7 December 1908, it served as a cinema, a bingo hall and a strip club. In its heyday such stars as Max Miller, Wee Georgie Wood, Sandy Powell, Vera Lynn, Gracie Fields, Laurel and Hardy and Morecambe and Wise all appeared there, as well as two comedians with a strong Birmingham connection, George Robey, 'the Prime Minister of Mirth' and Sid Field. When this picture was taken, Will Hay was bottom of the bill of the Aston Hippodrome, which meant he had second billing after the star of the show, Edna Latonne. (D.R. Harvey Collection)

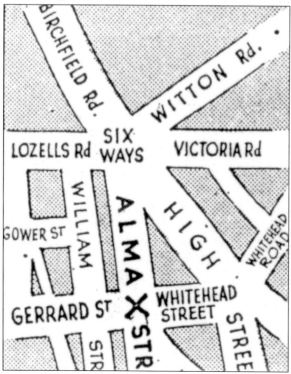

Major accidents involving buses were mercifully quite rare, but one did occur on 11 October 1963 at the junction of Whitehead Road and Alma Street. This involved a bus on the 7 route hitting an Inner Circle vehicle and causing it to turn over. 2437 (JOJ 437), a new-look-front Crossley-bodied Crossley DD42/7 was left lying on its offside and so badly damaged that it was used afterwards as a temporary 'turn-over' training vehicle. 2437 had the unfortunate distinction of being the first Crossley, out of 270 that were owned, to be withdrawn. Thankfully there were no fatalities in the accident, but fifty-three people were injured, four of whom were detained at Birmingham's General Hospital. (D.R. Harvey Collection)

The Gunmaker's Arms on the corner of Gerrard and Wilton streets. The Gunmakers competed for trade with the other Gerrard Street locals, The Union and The Belle Vue. Ansells bought The Gunmaker's in 1892 for £1,860 and it was rebuilt around the turn of the century. It is a grade 2 listed building but unfortunately its magnificent bar has been stripped out by thieves. (Barbara Palmer)

On the opposite side of Gerrard Street from the Gunmaker's were the corner fish and chip shop of Mrs Spirou Michael and the terraced houses numbered 114 to 136 Gerrard Street. This shows the row shortly before it was demolished. (Public Works Department)

883 (BOP 883), a Metro-Cammell-bodied Daimler COG5, which entered service on 1 September 1936, is turning from Gerrard Street to pull up to the first stop in Nursery Road, on the corner of Berners Street, on its way towards Hockley. The prospective passengers are girls, with their domestic science teacher, from the nearby secondary school. They are standing next to their 'Home Organization' house, which had been bought by the school in order to train the girls in such delights as how to sweep a floor, make a bed, wash clothes and cook meals. The girls and their teacher are going for a picnic in a park as part of their domestic science course. (Birmingham Central Reference Library)

This is again the Home Organization class at the Gerrard Street extension of Lozells School, on this occasion preparing for a lifetime of Monday washdays. The youngster in the pram is Paul Carney.

The Gerrard Street entrance to Lozells Street school in February 1968.

The infants' entrance to Lozells School in 1974.

The staff of Lozells Street Girls School. This is one of a number of photographs deposited in Birmingham Central Library on behalf of Evelyn Dorney, a domestic science teacher at he school.

The Salvation Army Hall, Nursery Road in April 1975. The Hall has since been rebuilt. The spiritual needs of the residents of this part of Lozells were well catered for. The 8c has just passed the Lozells Methodist church on Gerrard Street and reached the Salvation Army Hall. Round the corner in Hunters road is St Mary's Roman Catholic Convent.

Another Crossley-bodied Daimler CVG6, 2802 (JOJ 802), overtakes an awkwardly parked scooter, as it turns from Nursery Road into Hunters Road. To the left of the bus is the early twentieth-century Carnegie Infant Welfare Institute while behind it is the St Mary's Convent High School. For many years Hunters Road was where the buses clocked in at the Bundy Clock on the inner ring of the 8 service at Hockley, though this was later moved to a lay-by opposite Hockley garage. 2802, a fifty-five seat bus, entered service on 1 July 1952 and until 1967 was allocated to Harborne garage. By this time the bus had been transferred to Liverpool Street garage. (R.F. Mack)

One of Liverpool Street garage's 'tin-front' Daimler buses, 2706 (JOJ 706), which entered service on 1 September 1951, appears from beneath the concrete gloom of Hockley Flyover around 1968. It is about to turn into Whitmore Street opposite Hockley bus garage when operating on the Inner Circle route. The bus working on the 72 route to The Hawthorns is a later Crossley-bodied Daimler CVG6, while the bus on the 8 is a Daimler-engined Daimler. Hockley Flyover was finally opened for traffic in the same year as the buses pass beneath its concrete span. (R.F. Mack)

On Friday 31 March 1939, three trams, led by U.E.C.-built eight-wheeled car 548 working on the 26 service from Oxhill Road, travel down Soho Hill towards Hockley Brook. To the left are the tracks which lead to Hockley depot. To the right, just in front of the unloading tramcar, is a Smethwick-registered Standard Flying Ten. By the end of this weekend, the trams would be no more and by the 1960s this apparently prosperous shopping centre would be wiped out to be replaced by Hockley Flyover. (H.B. Priestley)

In the summer of 1958 another Metro-Cammell-bodied Daimler CVD6, 2660 (JOJ 660), which originally entered service to replace the Coventry Road trolleybus in June 1951, travels along Whitmore Street passing the entrance to Hockley garage on the right. It is working on the clockwise outer ring of the Inner Circle and heads towards Aston Cross. Usually the Inner Circle worked along Heaton Street, but as this and Ford Street were closed, the 8 route came past the Soho Pool railway wharf, overtaking the parked Vauxhall LIX Wyvern. The bus garage seems to contain only Leyland-bodied Leyland PD2/1s from the 2131-2180 class which dated from 1949, including 2162 and 2163. (R.F. Mack)

After the roads around the Hockley flyover redevelopment scheme were built, many of the old street patterns were swept away. The bus garage is the complex of buildings to the right, above the Ford Zephyr 4 saloon which is turning from Hockley Circus into Icknield Street with its new bus lay-by. Within a few years the Inner Circle as well as all the other road traffic would use the improved and widened Heaton Street, but that was only after the underpass beneath Hockley Hill was eventually brought into use. 2715 (JOJ 715), a Daimler-engined Daimler with a fifty-four seat M.C.C.W. body, waits to pull out into the traffic during 1968. (M.R. Keeley)

The civil engineering work to construct the flyover at Hockley Brook began in the mid-1960s with the clearing of many of the old properties and leaving blocks of concrete in fenced-off yards awaiting placing in the jig-saw of the new road network. The old Hockley Brook shopping area had been in terminal decline since the mid-1950s and was finally swept away in the next decade. On the distant skyline, as a reminder of the 'ancient regime', is the 1868-built spire of St Michael's church in Soho Hill, while in the centre of the scene is the original City of Birmingham Tramways Company steam tram depot of 1888, which survives today as Travel West Midland's Hockley garage. Recalling a grimmer Victorian age is the three-storied housing in Whitmors Street which had already been partially abandoned. On the right is one of Hockley garage's MOF-registered Daimler CVG6s with a Crossley body. It is negotiating the road works when working on the 90 service to Kingstanding on 16 March 1967. (Birmingham Central Reference Library)

Six

Icknield Street
to Spring Hill

Icknield Street School building, August 1972. A starred grade 2 listed building. The school opened in 1883 with capacity for 870 pupils. The school was designed by Martin and Chamberlain, architects to the Birmingham School Board, and like nearly all of their schools was 'the best building in the neighbourhood'. Part of the now largely deserted building is the Bagram Ashram Centre.

1872 (HOV 872), is travelling along Icknield Street towards Spring Hill in April 1964. It is coming out of the one way street system and is about to cross the Lodge Road and Key Hill junction. To the left of the Daimler CVG6 are commercial premises. John James was an electrical retailer who had many outlets in the Birmingham area, reaching its most profitable period in the late 1960s. A Servis washing machine with attached mangles stands at the shop's entrance while inside, fridges cost £35 each and a spherical 'Sputnik'-style Hoover vacuum cleaner just behind the Belisha Beacon is also available. (D.R. Harvey Collection)

The impressive late Victorian commercial buildings stood on the north side of Lodge Road dominating the corner with Icknield Street. The Inner Circle bus route passed along Icknield Street and the Lodge Road stop was a fare stage, as indicated on the 'flag' just below the 'Jeanne' shop sign. This corner site was dominated by Poole's electrical shop, who were daring to stay open until 7 p.m. on Fridays, and in 1952 were offering 'Easy Terms' on the payment of electrical goods. Poole's shop would be taken over by the much more aggressively-styled John James chain of electrical shops a few years later. Next door were the premises of Freeman, Hardy and Willis shoe shop, Mr Mellow's grocers shop and Glarry's Gown Shop. (Birmingham Central Reference Library)

Hockley Pentescostal church on Lodge Road. Although Lodge Road is just off the route the church is very visible from the 8 route, usually displaying the message 'Meet the Author of the World's Best Selling Book Every Sunday'. Further along Lodge Road is the Inner Circle café – recognition of the route at last!

The Bulls Head, at the corner of Key Hill and Icknield Street, c. 1920. The tenants were Tom Rowland and Alice Lewis. This three-storey nineteenth-century pub, with its splendid corner light, closed in 1984.

The early-wartime Morrison electric milk float owned by the Midland Counties Dairy Company manages to obscure the barely visible Icknield Street railway bridge, and 1866 (HOV 866) pulls away from the stop outside the premises of the Centric Cycle Company in May 1964. Next to the road sign is the entrance to the Caves brassfoundry, who specialized in display stands. All of the well-maintained three-storied shops in Icknield Street were to be demolished in the 1970s. The bus would turn left from Icknield Street into Lodge Road just beyond the parked Austin A40 saloon. (J.H. Taylforth Collection)

Great Western Inn, a typical corner-sited three-storey Victorian pub.

In February 1984, a West Midlands P.T.E. Daimler 'Fleetline' CRG6LX 4324 (NOB 324M), one of a batch of Park Royal-bodied buses which entered service in September 1973, passes Pitsford Street along Icknield Street. The standard W.M.P.T.E. double-decker was built to a height of 14' 2½", so that they could safely be driven beneath bridges such as Icknield Street (14' 3" high). By this time, the former G.W.R. railway line linking Birmingham, Snow Hill to Wolverhampton Low Level over Icknield Street was disused although the infrastructure was kept intact for possible future use. The imposing Hockley goods shed building was just a small part of the Hockley goods station which was developed in the late nineteenth century and completed by 1912. The bridge over Icknield Street was in fact two bridges, effectively forming a 125-yard-long tunnel beneath the main-line, on the far side and the goods lines into Hockley Port. (D.R. Harvey)

Only the new bridge, constructed on the line of the old Great Western route between Birmingham and Wolverhampton, crosses Icknield Street today. This carries the Midland Metro, the light railway system which opened on 30 May 1999. When the Metro was being built, some of the original burial grounds in Key Hill cemetery were disturbed, resulting in the reburial of a number of 200-year-old coffins. The dual carriageway that is today's Icknield Street, is no longer traversed by the Inner Circle bus route, which was diverted to pass through the busier Jewellery Quarter, in nearby Vyse Street. (D.R. Harvey)

The chapel of Key Hill cemetery, August 1961. The first of the two neighbouring city cemeteries on the route. Key Hill, originally the General Cemetery, was the cemetery for Dissenters, Warstone Lane for the Church of England. The chapel was designed by Charles Edge. It was demolished in 1966.

Warstone Lane cemetery looking toward Icknield Street in 1953. The second of the Jewellery Quarter cemeteries opened in 1848. It has an impressive blue brick gatehouse in Warstone Lane. The cemetery is best known for its catacombs. (Birmingham Parks Department)

Icknield Street was rare in that its premises were numbered consecutively down the east side and then back up the west side. Icknield Street was part of the Roman Rykrield Street which ran from the south to Wall, the legion's staging post of Letocetum, near Lichfield. Occupying the corner of Hingeston Street was The Royal Mint, an Atkinson-owned public house which was briefly managed by the parents of the Birmingham-born actor Tony Britton. Hingeston Street was where the tortuous Lodge Road 32 tram service crossed Icknield Street on its way to Lodge Road and Winson Green. The pub was almost opposite the Birmingham Mint, which celebrated its centenary in 1989. 2797 (JOJ 797), a 1952 Daimler CVG6 with a Crossley H30/25R body stands outside Sydney Tibbatts 'dining rooms' while beyond the tipper lorry is The Royal Oak, owned by Mitchells & Butlers. (D.R. Harvey Collection)

The Birmingham Mint in Icknield Street. There has been little alteration to this building since it was first built for Ralph Heaton in 1862. It was then called Heaton's Mint before, in 1899, becoming the Birmingham Mint, the largest privately-owned mint in the world.

Brighton Place, opposite the Mint on Icknield Street. The block was built in 1872 and the entry led to a courtyard of back-to-backs. The 'Now Open' sign of the shop seems a little optimistic as this was just prior to demolition of these buildings.

Great Western Terrace on Icknield Street between Hingeston and Prescott streets, close to the Royal Oak Public House, in the early 1970s.

The present-day Inner Circle bus route leaves Icknield Street and turns up Warstone Lane to arrive at the lovingly restored Chamberlain Clock at the junction with Vyse Street. The clock was unveiled in January 1904 as a token of thanks to Joseph Chamberlain. He had supported the successful abolition of plate duties, which had sorely affected the profitability of the late Victorian jewellery trade in Hockley. The bus is 1696 (V 696 MOA), a 43-seater Mercedes-Benz 0405N pictured on 25 May 2002. Behind the bus is the lodge to Warstone Cemetery while alongside is the HSBC Bank, opened by the Midland in 1892 and decorated over the front door with a statue and stone carving associated with Henry Vyse's coat of arms. The Rosa Villa public house, on the corner of Warstone Lane and Vyse Street, was used by jewellery employers on paydays to pass over the worker's wages. Despite its antiquarian appearance, the Rosa Villa Tavern was built in 1919. (D.R. Harvey)

Travelling along Vyse Street towards the Chamberlain Clock is 2709 (A709 UOE), an M.C.W. Metrobus MK II, working on the 8A route. Years before the route was diverted into the Jewellery Quarter, Vyse Street's only bus service was the 19, City Circle service. The Jewellery Quarter of Birmingham was built on land owned by the Vyse family and manufacture of gold products rapidly expanded in the area due to the amount of cheap gold available after the Californian gold rush of 1849. Much of the Jewellery Quarter was located in converted domestic premises but those next to The Rose Villa public house were replaced in the 1990s with a purpose-built set of jeweller's shops which stand in the shadow of the 1960s flatted factory known as The Peg. (D.R. Harvey)

A stretch of small shops in Icknield Street between the library and the Warstone Inn, on the right. This row of shops was soon to be replaced by the Brookfield Shopping Centre, which itself has now been demolished after many years of decline and dereliction.

Seven

Completing the Circle: Spring Hill to Five Ways

On 16 March 1949, an Inner Circle bus passing from Monument Road into Icknield Street, was hit by a fire engine and finished up in the non-fiction shelves of Spring Hill library. This was one of the worst accidents in the history of municipal public transport in Birmingham, with ten passengers being killed. 1041 (CVP 141), a Daimler COG5 of 1937, had its offside lower saloon ripped out in the accident and as a result was scrapped. Here the fire brigade have hosed down the cobbled road surface to wash away the fuel oil which was spilled after the diesel tank in the bus ruptured. In front of the bus is a solitary Austin Ten police car. Off to the right, the former bus 92 (MV 489), A.E.C 'Renown', which had been converted to a mobile crane, waits to lift the stricken 1041 back onto its wheels again, prior to being towed away and subsequently broken up. (Birmingham Central Reference Library)

Just leaving the bus shelter opposite Spring Hill Library is a very smart-looking 1937-built Daimler COG5 fitted with a Metro-Cammell fifty-four seater body. It is 1959 and 1008 (CVP 108) is enjoying a brief return to service between 1958 and 1960. By now the bus had been fitted with trafficators, which on the nearside is the black box just above the nearside side light. In the background is the Spring Hill junction with Dudley Road running at right angles across the Icknield Street and Monument Road junction. (R.F. Mack)

The driver of the quiet-engined Daimler CVD6 pulls away from the traffic lights in Icknield Street. To the right is the terracotta and brick-built Spring Hill Library which opened in 1893 in Gothic revival ecclesiastical style. Behind the bus is the chimney of St George's aluminium hollow-ware factory owned by Bulpitt's, which was on the corner of Camden Street. The bus is 2714 (JOJ 714), which in 1956 still had its full-length front wings. (R.H.G. Simpson)

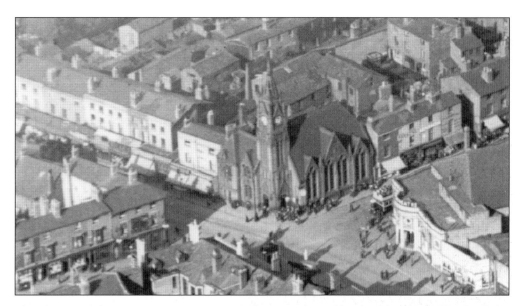

The sheer awfulness of 1920s inner Birmingham can be well judged by the acres of tightly-packed back-to-back houses and courtyards. These unsanitary dwellings survived for another forty years. One of Birmingham Corporation's open-topped, outside-staircased A.E.C. 503s, fitted with a fifty-four seat body built by Brush in 1923, waits to cross Spring Hill at the library during the first days of the infant and probably incomplete Inner Circle route. These buses were numbered 60-71 and 89-90 and lasted until 1930, but were never fitted with pneumatic tyres or top-covers. To the nearside of the bus, in Summerhill Road is the Palace Theatre. (Birmingham Central Reference Library)

The interior of the Palace Cinema, shortly after becoming a cinema on 18 December 1911. The cinema, across the road from the library, started life as a variety theatre in 1905, switching to a cinema six years later. Its impressive interior could seat 861 people. The Palace closed in 1941, after which the building was used by Bulpits until it was demolished in 1981. The site is currently being redeveloped.

Spring Hill Library. The closest community or branch library, as they used to be known, to the city centre. It caters for the needs of the residents of Ladywood, although the dereliction of the Brookfield centre has left it isolated. The library, a listed building, has survived plans both to demolish it and to move it wholesale to another site. The magnificent interior (below) has benefited from a recent refurbishment.

The Station Inn on the corner of Monument Road and Cope Street in 1960. It first opened in 1854 and closed in 1965. Beyond it are the typical three-storied Victorian houses which survived in the area until the mid-1960s.

Metro-Cammell-bodied Daimler CVD6 2714 (JOJ 714) is pictured again, though this time in Monument Road, with Icknield Square and Leach Street in the background. The driver, in his summer khaki jacket, moves swiftly towards his cab, having just 'pegged' the Bundy Clock which was located on the railway bridge just above Monument Lane Station on the old L.N.W.R. route to the north-west. (N.N. Forbes)

From the left, the Bundy Clock, a fine Victorian men's urinal, The Bridge Inn, Monument Road post office and Pearce Bros, house furnishers. The Bridge Inn was originally in Icknield Street West and moved to Monument Road around 1877. It closed in 1967.

An exposed-radiator, HOV-registered Daimler CVG6, stands on the bridge over the Birmingham Canal in Monument Road, clocking-in at the Bundy Clock. Behind the bus are some of the three-storied courtyard terraces dating from the 1850s which had been earmarked for demolition immediately after the end of the Second World War. These houses were demolished under the redevelopment scheme which dramatically altered the Ladywood landscape in the 1960s. The new factory on the left was in Ledsam Street. It was the new machine shop belonging to Belliss & Morcom's mechanical engineering company that opened in 1953, but closed soon afterwards in 1961. (D.R. Harvey Collection)

The Duke of Wellington on the corner of Leach Street and Monument Road in 1954, with the local shops next door

The Social Club domino team playing in a match in the Duke of Wellington in 1947. The team were strong competitors in the Ladywood League, another example of the sense of community centred around the local corner pub. This would be lost when the pub closed with the wholesale redevelopment of the area in the sixties.

Monument Road Baths. The baths officially opened on 27 June 1940 replacing the original corporation baths on the site which dated from 1883. The new baths were demolished in 1974 due to structural faults. In their heyday the baths were used by top swimmers including the Olympic medallist Nick Gillingham.

The junction of Monument Road and Wood Street in 1959. The corner shops, Pearks, were part of a Birmingham-based grocers chain which at this date had 52 branches across the city. The advert for Barbers Teas is a reminder of another local connection – Barber's Tea Company was based in the city centre in Pershore Street.

Co-op shops at 133–136 Monument Road between Johnstone Street and Wood Street, almost opposite the swimming baths.

The Inner Circle bus route, after crossing Icknield Port Road, arrived at Ladywood Road. An eight-wheeled air-braked tram, 749, built by Brush in 1926, picks up passengers on its way towards Five Ways. On the left corner, next to the utility tram shelter, are the premises of Thomas Furber & Sons. They were undertakers established in 1868. The woman who is striding across the tram tracks is heading towards Chamberlain Gardens which were opened by local MP Neville Chamberlain, on 28 June 1924. It was one of the few patches of greenery on the Inner Circle bus route. (J.S.Webb)

2146 (JOJ 146) speeds along an almost deserted Monument Road near Ladywood Road while working the Inner Circle route. It is being followed by a wrap-round windscreen Vauxhall Victor F series. The bus is one of Hockley garage's Leyland-bodied Leyland 'Titan' PD2/1s of 1949 vintage. It is travelling away from the Ivy Bush and Hagley Road and is speeding through one of the rarer arboreal sections of Monument Road. The bus survived in service until December 1968, by which time the Vauxhall might well have rusted away. (A.D. Broughall)

One of the splendid houses on Monument Road, number 172 in August 1959. The house was then being used as a surgery by Dr Leszek Ostrowski.

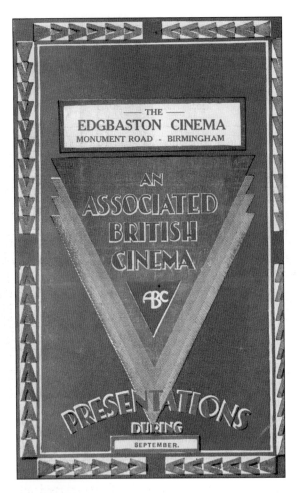

THE
EDGBASTON CINEMA
MONUMENT ROAD - BIRMINGHAM

AN
ASSOCIATED
BRITISH
CINEMA
ABC

PRESENTATIONS
DURING
SEPTEMBER.

The Edgbaston ABC at 233-235 Monument Road between Parker Street and Bellis Road. The cinema opened on Christmas Eve 1924. It was a large suburban house with seating for 1,616 people. The programme for the week beginning 2 September 1935 featured Marlene Dietrich in *The Devil is a Woman* and Douglas Fairbanks and Gertrude Lawrence in *Mimi*. The cinema closed on 16 November 1968, the last film shown was *Camelot*. Like many cinemas at this date it then became a bingo hall and was subsequently demolished.

The tram service along Hagley Road was vigorously resisted by the residents of the Calthorpe Estate who did not want 'the unsightly overhead' lines over their arborealy rich main road. The trams arrived in February 1914 (including a first-class service for three months) and departed in 1930. A 512 class bogie car, with open balconies is passing the Roman Catholic Oratory church of the Immaculate Conception, better known as the Oratory. The Gothic-style houses on the corner of Plough & Harrow Road, belonging to the church, were built between 1903 and 1909, to the designs of E. Doran Webb as a memorial to Cardinal Henry Newman. (Commercial Postcard)

Opposite: Waiting to cross Hagley Road from Vicarage Road, when working on the 8 route towards Hockley is 3165 (MOF 165), a Daimler CVG6 with a Crossley H30/25R body. The Regency row of buildings, which includes the Ivy Bush public house, have survived as retail outlets at the junction at Monument Road. The Inner Circle route has been protected at this busy junction by traffic lights, at which 3165 is waiting, in about 1968, judging by the almost new Sunbeam Rapier on the right. (Birmingham Central Reference Library)

The vaguely Jacobean-styled Plough & Harrow Hotel stands alongside the Oratory church in Plough & Harrow Road, which is still used by the Inner Circle bus route today as an important one-way link between Monument Road and Hagley Road. The ivy-covered Plough & Harrow Hotel was listed as a public house as late as the 1890s, but was one of the first hotels along Hagley Road which today grace the road in abundance. (Birmingham Central Reference Library)

Travelling along Harborne Road, Edgbaston, lined with large, late Regency and early Victorian villas, working on the 8 route around 1965 is 1907 (HOV 907). This is an exposed-radiator Daimler CVG6 with a M.C.C.W. H30/24R body, dating from May 1949. It is travelling towards the Ivy Bush. The houses in Harborne Road were part of the Calthorpe Estate, a sizeable area of the emerging Victorian Birmingham which was resolutely middle class. The land developed by the Calthorpe family was to the windward of the noise, dirt and 'noxious vapours' produced by industry and by 1870 much of Edgbaston had become, according to Francis Brett Young 'a region of tree-lined roads and exquisitely tasteful houses'. (A.D. Broughall)

Eight

The Inner Circle
Bus Garages

Hockley depot was built for the Birmingham Central Tramways Company for their cable cars which began operation from Colmore Row to Hockley Brook on 24 March 1888 and extended, on a second cable, to the New Inns on 21 April 1889. The BCT depot housed fifty-three cable cars and the service continued until Friday 30 June 1911, when the twenty-one-year lease expired. When the Soho Road services finally converted to electric tramcar operation, the depot was re-opened on 12 June 1912, having doubled in size, with eight roads and a capacity for eighty-eight trams. In the summer of 1938, U.E.C.-bodied bogie tramcar 546 of 1913 stands on the forecourt siding leading to the stationery and ticket office, while car 615, which was built by Brush in 1920, stands at the entrance to the depot's Road 1. (R.T. Coxon)

After the tram routes to West Bromwich, Wednesbury and Dudley closed down on 1 April 1939, Hockley depot was converted to motor bus operation, with further covered accommodation being added. The Soho Road trams were replaced by all eighty-five of the EOG-registered, Metro-Cammell-bodied torque converter Leyland 'Titan' TD6cs numbered 211-295. Within weeks of the declaration of war, the Leyland-bodied 1270-1319, with corresponding FOF registrations, were allocated to Hockley garage for the Dudley Road tram replacement services. The heavy air raid on 22 November 1940 reduced this virtually new stock of buses to this twisted mass of burnt-out bus body frames yet only six never ran again! (D.R. Harvey Collection)

The end of hostilities saw the introduction of new buses to Hockley and other corporation garages. A brand new 1897 (HOV 897) stands on Hockley garage forecourt on 25 March 1949, just delivered from Metro-Cammell. Although Hockley was an operator of the Inner Circle route, this bus was not allocated there, instead entering service from Barford Street and latterly from Liverpool Street garage. To the right is an EOG-registered Leyland 'Titan' TD6cs which after having its original M.C.C.W. body destroyed in the 1940 air-raid, was rebuilt with a curvaceous English Electric body intended for Manchester Corporation. On the right, hidden by the Fordson E83W van of 1849 vintage, is a petrol-engined A.E.C. 'Regent' dating from around 1930, one of fifty to receive a 'utility' body built to stringent wartime standards by Brush Engineering of Loughborough. (S. Palmer)

Rosebery Street, just off Dudley Road, was the second corporation tram depot to be opened after Miller Street. The depot opened on 14 April 1906 and had a capacity for eighty-five trams, although this figure was only realised after B.M.T.'s tramway lease expired on 1 April 1928 and the Dudley Road's tram services became operated by the corporation. Thus there was no space for bus operation until the closure of the Ladywood and Lodge Road tram routes after 30 August 1947. The premises were converted into a bus garage, initially to work the Dudley Road services. In early 1950, about the last thirty-two Park Royal-bodied Leyland 'Titan' PD2/1s were allocated to Rosebery Street for nearly their entire lives, although after closure on 29 June 1968, some went to Quinton garage. Four Leylands, with exposed chromed radiators and one Daimler CVD6 wait either as spares or awaiting maintenance. (L. Mason)

The dreaded white-coated garage foreman walks in front of two of the garage's Daimler CVD6s, while a mechanic manoeuvres his way out of the cab of 2212 (JOJ 212). The bus is one of the thirty-two Leyland 'Titan' PD2/1s with a London-built Park Royal H29/25R body. It entered service on 1 February 1950 and spent its sixteen-year life working from Rosebery Street. With the exception of a Leyland 'Atlantean' demonstrator, 460 MTE, Rosebery Street's only other buses were the last twenty of the 1952 batch of 'tin-fronted' Daimler CVD6s, which, unlike the Leylands, did appear on the Inner Circle route quite regularly. (B.W. Ware)

Above: Barford Street, converted from a factory and opened in June 1925, was the first corporation bus garage, very soon assuming control for operating the Inner Circle. All the A.D.C. 507 low-height 'pick-pocket specials' were operated by Barford Street, although Daimler COG5s and a batch of wartime Guy 'Arab' IIs were allocated there until 1948/49. 1621, 1622 and the subtly different 1630 wait for another tour of duty in 1954, and just visible is a 1952 Crossley-bodied Daimler CVG6, which was one of nineteen added to the garage's establishment for a brief three-year sojourn. The garage closed in April 1955 when its work was re-allocated due to the opening of Lea Hall garage. (W.A. Camwell)

When Liverpool Street garage opened in September 1936, it had an initial allocation of 150 buses. There was a fleet of new BOP-registered Daimler COG5s of which 846 (BOP 846) was one, remaining at the garage until the Second World War. The garage was responsible for just under half of the buses working on the Inner Circle bus route. 846 is being refuelled at the diesel pumps, while another Metro-Cammell bodied COG5, 854 is on the left. Between them is 819 (BOP 819), which had a Birmingham Railway Carriage & Wagon body, distinguishable from the rear by the subtly different curve over the rear platform. (D.R. Harvey Collection)

Opposite: Standing over the pits in Liverpool Street garage in September 1936 is 862 (BOP 862), another one of the Metro-Cammell bodied Daimler COG5s which entered service from this garage when it was first opened. Two buses from the same batch, 848 and 851, are parked to the right. Just visible on the right is one of the A.D.C 507s with outside staircase Short Brothers-built bodywork. The forty-two buses were numbered 296-337, and had entered service in 1928. The A.D.C. design was outdated within eighteen months of delivery and were by this time 'on their last legs', all were withdrawn in the summer of 1937. (B.C.T. Collection)

Above: The conductor stands on the platform of 2441 (JOJ 441) and prepares for a bouncy journey on the stiff-sprung Crossley DD42/7 from Liverpool Street garage by way of the Adderley Street exit. The bus, with its driver-testing synchromesh-gearbox, would have been about sixteen years old at this time, around 1966. The bus has the black waistrail fleet numbers that first appeared in 1962. In the background, on the right, is 1862 (HOV 862), an exposed-radiator Daimler CVG6 that was not withdrawn until February 1968, by which time rear-engined buses were beginning to appear on the Inner Circle route. (PhotoFives)

A typical mix of Highgate Road's buses in 1959 included three Daimler COG5s, with 1069 (CVP 169) at the head of one line of parked buses, four exposed-radiatored Daimler CVG6s of 1949 and two 'tin-fronted' Daimler CVG6s with Crossley bodies, including 2888 (JOJ 888), hiding behind the column on the right. When running, the HOV-registered CVG6s always seemed noisier than the apparently sophisticated JOJ and MOF-registered examples. Although the pre-war COG5s lacked a cylinder, when running they had about the same performance and sounds as the 1948 and 1949 CVG6s and it was only when idling that their 'missing pot' seem noticeable. (R.F. Mack)

Left: Highgate Road was built as a tram depot on 25 November 1913 and lasted as the main provider of tramcars for the Stratford Road until that group of routes closed on 5 January 1937. Re-opening as a bus garage in June 1937, it was twice damaged during November 1940 by land mines; fifty-seven buses were damaged in the second raid, but most were back in service with wooden boards over the windows within a few days. All thirteen of these windowless and shrapnel-dented buses are 1936 or 1937-built Daimler COG5s with Metro-Cammell bodies. Highgate Road garage closed on 14 July 1962 and the premises were transferred to the fire and ambulance service as a main workshop. (J.H. Taylforth Collection)

A fitting finale. Representing all the conductors and drivers who have worked the inner circle, driver A.B. Dougan at the wheel of a double-decker in Gerrard Street, Lozells, in March 2002.

The authors researching the route, waiting for the 8C, which is a MkII Metrobus, near to The Gunmaker's Arms in Gerrard Street.